Twayne's English Authors Series

Sylvia E. Bowman, *General Editor*

INDIANA UNIVERSITY

Nahum Tate

TEAS 126

Nahum Tate

By CHRISTOPHER SPENCER

University of North Carolina at Greensboro

Twayne Publishers, Inc. :: New York

Library of Congress Catalog Card Number: 76-152014

MANUFACTURED IN THE UNITED STATES OF AMERICA

Preface

Nahum Tate, poet laureate of England from 1692 to 1715, was the author of more than one hundred published works, including several collaborations with John Dryden, a long-lived adaptation of William Shakespeare's *King Lear,* and an even more enduring metrical translation of the Psalms, which was widely used in churches until a century ago; yet no book-length study of his work has been published before this one. Some explanation of why none has appeared, as well as some other reasons why one should be published, are suggested in the first chapter.

However, this book has been preceded by several useful doctoral dissertations: much of the initial mapping out of the subject was done in the comprehensive dissertations of H. F. Scott-Thomas (Johns Hopkins, 1932) and Samuel A. Golden (Trinity College, Dublin, 1954). The second is especially valuable for its information about Tate's attendance at Trinity College. Other dissertations that have been helpful are those of A. H. Scouten on *A Duke and No Duke* (Louisiana State University, 1942), James B. Ayres on Tate's Shakespearean adaptations (Ohio State University, 1964), and Ruth McGugan on *The Ingratitude of a Common-Wealth* (University of Illinois, 1965).

During the Restoration period, Tate was one of the chief adapters of the plays of Shakespeare and other Elizabethan dramatists. After editing several of these Restoration adaptations, I wanted to make a critical study of them; but I found that knowledge about Tate was insufficient for the purpose and that I would have to conduct my own investigation of the man and his work in order to supply the background necessary for the critical study; this book grew out of my efforts to assemble this knowledge.

Since Tate is better known by his reputation than by his writings, the chapter on his life is preceded by a short chapter on his fame. The three chapters on the plays and adaptations (Four, Five, and Six) are preceded and followed by discussions of the early and the late poems. The last two chapters are on Tate's major semiliterary effort, the *New Version of the Psalms,* and his mock-heroic on tea, sometimes considered his best poem. The bibliography contains a list of Tate's works, in which I have recorded all of his writings that I have been able to find.

I wish to thank Professors Scouten and Golden for sending me offprints, and Dr. McGugan for lending me microfilm. I am grateful to the Committee on Research Grants of Illinois State University for helping to support the research that went into this book. And, finally, I would thank my wife and children for their encouragement.

CHRISTOPHER SPENCER

The University of
North Carolina at Greensboro

Contents

Chronology

ca. 1652 Nahum Tate born, probably in Ireland.

1668 In June, entered Trinity College, Dublin, with his brother Faithful.

1672 Bachelor of Arts, Trinity College, Dublin.

1676 About November, published his first poem in Flatman's *Poems and Songs* and had his first volume (*Poems*) ready for publication.

1677 About February, *Poems* published.

1678 About June, *Brutus of Alba* performed at Dorset Garden.

1680 Collaborated with Dryden and others in Ovid's *Epistles*. In December (again in January, 1681), *The History of King Richard the Second* banned at Drury Lane.

1681 *The History of King Lear* performed at Dorset Garden. About December, *The Ingratitude of a Common-Wealth* performed at Drury Lane.

1682 In November, *The Second Part of Absalom and Achitophel* published.

1684 About May, the second edition of *Poems* published. In August, *A Duke and No Duke* performed at Drury Lane.

1685 Wrote the "Song for St. Cecilia's Day," November 22.

1689 Purcell's *Dido and Aeneas* (for which Tate wrote the libretto) first performed.

1690 About February, praised King William in *A Pastoral Dialogue*.

1692 In October, Juvenal's *Satires* published. In December, appointed poet laureate.

1694 In January, University of Dublin centenary Ode performed.

1695 Elegies on Archbishop Tillotson and Queen Mary published.

1696 With Nicholas Brady, published *A New Version of the Psalms of David,* dedicated to William.
1698 About May, the *New Version* published in a substantially revised edition.
1699 *Elegies* published.
1700 Supplement to the *New Version* published; *Panacea: A Poem Upon Tea* published.
1701 Took King William's side against Parliament and praised the Kentish Petitioners.
1710 *An Essay for Promoting of Psalmody* published in answer to criticism of the *New Version.*
1713 In March and April, edited *The Monitor* with "M. Smith."
1715 Wrote the Song for King George I's birthday (May 28). On July 30, died in the Mint; on August 1, was buried at Saint George's Church, Southwark.

CHAPTER 1

Fame's Brass Trumpet

IN CHAUCER'S *House of Fame* the Goddess Fame is visited by nine groups of petitioners, some of whom desire her gift and some of whom do not. To the various groups she awards good fame, blown abroad through a golden trumpet, or ill fame, circulated through a brass trumpet, or simply oblivion; but her choice is independent of the petitioners' merit and is entirely a matter of whim. For Nahum Tate, Fame seems to have assigned the cruel and undeserved fate of having just enough ill fame for historians of literature to say that he merited oblivion.

This opinion originated with Tate's younger contemporaries. In the Dedication to Prince Posterity in Jonathan Swift's *Tale of a Tub* (1704), His Highness is assured ironically that the age does have learning, politeness, and wit; John Dryden's *Virgil* can perhaps be found, and "there is another, call'd Nahum Tate, who is ready to make Oath that he has caused many Rheams of Verse to be published, whereof both himself and his Bookseller (if lawfully required) can still produce authentick Copies, and therefore wonders why the World is pleased to make such a Secret of it."[1] In "The Book-Worm," Thomas Parnell, the friend of Swift and Alexander Pope, used pages from Tate and Thomas Shadwell to clean the altar after the worm had been sacrificed, observing that he had not "miss'd [their] works till now" and that this was the only way in which the two poets could please the Muses.

And in his *Epistle to Dr. Arbuthnot,* Pope described varieties of barren poets and declared that "nine such Poets made a Tate." He alluded to "Tate's poor page" in the earlier *Dunciad;* and in the later version, when the hero had become Colley Cibber, the current poet laureate, Pope referred to "the mild Limbo of our

Father Tate" and bracketed him with Shadwell.[2] Samuel Johnson did not write a life of Tate, although he approved of the happy ending for *King Lear.* Sir Walter Scott considered Tate "one of those second-rate bards, who, by dint of pleonasm and expletive, can find smooth lines if any one will supply them with ideas." The Romantic critics disapproved emphatically of Tate's work as an adapter of Shakespeare, and by 1850 the word "Tatefication" had been invented to refer to the debasement of great literary works.[3] The modern view, which inherits this tradition, agrees that Tate's writings are "dull" and that they justify the word "Tatefication" coined from his name.

Of the three notorious laureates, Shadwell's reputation has been rehabilitated in recent years, and good things have been said of Cibber; but Tate has remained in the "mild Limbo" to which Pope and Fame assigned him. Actually, some of his contemporaries had a better opinion of him. In *The Athenian Mercury* for May 29, 1694, an anonymous writer praised Tate's recent *Poem on the Late Promotion* in lines as fluent as the ease he attributed to the author:

> If Nature's self wou'd write she'd learn of Thee
> So pure thy Style, thy Words so just and free,
> In all a charming Air of Modestie.
> Thy easy Numbers, soft as Love, present
> Chains, not of Slavery, but of Ornament:
> The willing Words in decent Order flow,
> Of each we say it cou'd not but be so.
> With such a pow'rful, yet a gentle sway
> High Heav'n commands, and all the World obey.

Others agreed: the dramatic biographer and critic Gerard Langbaine "allow'd [Tate] to be a Man of Wit and Parts";[4] and Samuel Wesley, the father of the founder of Methodism, praised both the man and his verse:

> For smooth and well turn'd Lines we T[ate] admire,
> Who has in Justness what he wants in Fire:
> Each Rhime, each Syllable well-weigh'd and fair,
> His Life and Manners scarce more regular.[5]

In modern times A. W. Ward, who called Tate "a painstaking

and talented writer" and praised him for "being able to accommodate himself to diverse styles," is one of the few historians of literature to speak well of Tate.[6] This evaluation is more nearly accurate than that of Swift and Pope and their successors: although Tate's work lacks the larger vision and energy of Dryden's, it has such other virtues as variety, adaptability, ingenuity, and fluency. His adaptations, imitations, and translations were almost always intelligently conceived and carried through, and many were deservedly successful.

Tate's work also has historical importance. Born during the Commonwealth, he wrote in the reigns of Charles II, James II, William III, Anne, and George I; he was poet laureate for twenty-three years, a period consisting of the entire reign of Queen Anne and parts of two other reigns. Among his dramatic works were his adaptation of *King Lear,* which became one of the most popular plays on the English stage and was performed for a period of one hundred and fifty years; *A Duke and No Duke,* a highly popular farce that remained on the stage for over half a century; and the libretto for Henry Purcell's music in *Dido and Aeneas.* Among Tate's poems were *The Second Part of Absalom and Achitophel;* a collection of short poems, many of which are in the tradition of melancholy verse; and a number of political and eulogistic poems, some of which at least had the distinction of going through several editions.

Among his translations were collaborations with Dryden and others in Ovid's *Epistles* and Juvenal's *Satires,* to both of which Tate contributed more than any other poet except Dryden himself. He also collaborated with Nicholas Brady in the *New Version of the Psalms of David* and in the *Supplement* to it. The former, widely used in Anglican and Episcopal churches until the middle of the nineteenth century, was published in over three hundred editions; several of the Tate-Brady "hymns" are to be found in almost every hymnal today, the best-known being "While shepherds watched their flocks." As critic, Tate seems to have appreciated Shakespeare better than almost any other Restoration writer except Dryden. He was also an early admirer of John Milton's minor poems as well as of *Paradise Lost,* and his admiration and imitation of Edmund Spenser were unusual for his time. Finally, Tate's career is of interest because he came from the generation between Dryden and Pope and because he lived in a literary world that was changing from the patronage system to dependence on a wider public. As Amy Reed has acknowledged, Tate "must be regarded as influential at the end of the century, because of his public position as laureate after Shadwell, and because the miscellaneous character of his literary activities brought him into contact with so many other writers."[7]

Tate's limitations are largely the results of his character. In 1753, Theophilus Cibber's *Lives of the Poets* described him as "a man of learning, courteous and candid" but as "a man of extreme modesty"; and David Baker's *Biographia Dramatica* (1782) cited opinions of three of Tate's contemporaries: Charles Gildon, who referred to him "as a man of great honesty and modesty; but he seems to have been ill qualified to advance himself in the world"; an unnamed "person who died in 1763, at the age of ninety, [who] remembered him well, and said he was remarkable for a downcast-look, and had seldom much to say for himself"; and William Oldys, the antiquary, who is cited as saying that Tate was "a free, good-natured, fuddling companion."[8] "Fuddling" normally implies drinking; and this observation, together with the custom of mentioning Tate with the hard-drinking Shadwell, seems responsible for the assertion, not independently supported and probably not true, that he was a heavy drinker. Scott-Thomas points out that Tate himself said he had a weak constitution; and there is additional support for this view in that four of Tate's works, from four different decades of his career, were dedicated to eminent London physicians (Walter Needham, 1677; Dr. Hobbs, 1686; Phineas Fowke, 1699; and William Gibbons, 1708).[9] In any event, most of the comments about him, the evidence of his career, and the impression given by his writings agree in suggesting a quiet and overly modest man who, in an aggressive, journalistic age, was inclined to avoid rather than begin or join controversies.

In 1934 Scott-Thomas published an essay which is still the only substantial study in print of Tate's work as a whole in relation to his time; in it, he maintains that Tate was essentially more of the past and the future (the Elizabethan age and the times of Young and Gray) than of the period of Dryden and Pope and that, in submitting himself to the demands of his age, he "was to his very finger-tips a thoroughgoing and unrepentant opportunist."[10] Scott-Thomas discusses Tate's close connections with the "moral trend" of the period and with Milton, and he concludes with a description of an unsuccessful poet moving unhappily from one failure to another because he was out of harmony with his time. But the evidence does not fit this conclusion: first, because a number of Tate's works were quite successful; second, because Tate's melancholy seems to have been mostly a matter of temperament rather than a result of the failures he did experience; and third, because Scott-Thomas's own evidence leads to a conclusion different from the one he draws.

The first half of Scott-Thomas's essay is devoted to examining Tate's works in terms of three "main tendencies of the era"—Neoclassicism, rationalism, and the scientific spirit. Attempting to show the absence of these in Tate's work, Scott-Thomas nevertheless found much of each—particularly the first and the third—in Tate and was driven to such summaries as the following: "in organization, language, and style, therefore, Tate felt and responded to the neo-classical stimulus. It was always unnatural to him, however, and though he practised the tenets with some degree of formal success, his heart never moved with his hand, and he never succeeded in acquitting himself with ease, spontaneity, or brilliance."[11] But Tate's responding to "the neo-classical stimulus" in "organization, language, and style" and his practicing these "tenets with some degree of formal success" show him to be very much of his age; if his work often lacked "ease, spontaneity, and brilliance," the deficiency was personal. Similarly, Scott-Thomas concludes that although "Tate's immediate connection with the scientific movement . . . was small . . . indirectly, he owed much to its attitude, outlook, and method, which frequently modified and shaped his work"; and his "prose style was fused in a scientific furnace."[12] In the second part of his essay, Scott-Thomas acknowledges but underestimates the importance of Tate's belonging to the moral movement of his day, of which more is said in later chapters of this study.

Tate was the kind of author who wrote well, though not brilliantly; and he was successful on the level of ingenious adaptation—though not on the level of creative originality—at combining many different influences. The evidence does not show that he would have been more at home in either the Elizabethan period or the mid-eighteenth century, except in the sense that a man of less aggressive character might have been more at home in a less aggressive literary age. Although there may be some validity to the charge of "opportunism" in a few of the works that Tate wrote before 1688, he followed thereafter the trend of the times without finding it inimical. As far as his interests, attitudes, and literary activities are concerned, it would have been hard to find a more suitable poet laureate for his age.

CHAPTER 2

Life

NAHUM TATE was born into a Puritan family that was associated with Trinity College, Dublin, and that had suffered severely from the vicissitudes of Ireland and England during the middle years of the seventeenth century. In 1641 the Irish Catholics rose in rebellion and massacred many of the English and Scottish settlers. One of the first to bring accounts of the rebellion to Dublin was the poet's grandfather, Faithful Teate, "D. D.," who had received his bachelor and master of arts degrees from Trinity College, Dublin (there is no actual record of his having been granted the doctor of divinity degree), and had served as rector in several parishes in Ireland. In October, 1641, he fled from his home in Ballyhays in County Cavan, bringing his family with him. He himself was stripped and robbed by the rebels on the way; two or three of his children died of the bad treatment they received; and the property he had left behind, worth almost four thousand pounds, was destroyed.

Shortly after Faithful Teate's arrival in Dublin he was appointed to replace temporarily the provost of Trinity College, who had fled to England when the rebellion began. From this position Teate was removed in April, 1643, charged with inefficiency and with being "ill affected unto the present established government under his Majesty's subjection."[1] He lived in England for several years (he was minister of the Cathedral Church of New Sarum in 1649 and was a minister in East Greenwich as late as 1657), but he returned to Ireland in 1658 at the invitation of Henry Cromwell and died there in the spring of 1660, survived by his widow; three or four sons (two were ministers, and one became a Junior Fellow of Trinity College), and one daughter, Mary, who married Thomas Parsons of London.[2]

His eldest son, Faithful Teate, born about 1627, attended Trinity College, Dublin; but he received his bachelor's and master's degrees from Cambridge. He married in 1640, and in the following year he succeeded his father-in-law as minister in Castle Camps. By 1651 he was minister at the churches of Saint Peter's and Saint Gregory's at Sudbury in Suffolk; and he was there in 1655 when, because of his "diligence," his living of one hundred pounds, which had been reduced to sixty pounds, was restored to its former level. He returned to Ireland about 1659, assigned at first to preach at Limerick; but a year later he was at Saint Werburgh's in Dublin. In June, 1661, he was prohibited from preaching because of having violated the Act of Uniformity.[3] He died in Ireland in late 1665 or 1666, survived by his wife Katherine; four sons, Faithful (born ca. 1651), Nahum, John, and Theophilus; and three daughters, Mary, Fidelia, and Ann.

Faithful Teate was also an author. The best known of his seven published works is *Ter Tria: or the Doctrine of the Three Sacred Persons, Father, Son & Spirit. Principal Graces, Faith, Hope, and Love. Main Duties, Prayer, Hearing, and Meditation. Summarily digested for the pleasure and profit of the Pious and Ingenious Reader,* which was published in London in 1658, appeared in a second edition in 1669 and was translated into German and published in Leipzig in 1698.[4] This poem of about fifty-seven hundred lines is strongly reminiscent of George Herbert in tone and ingenuity of stanza form. The poet is filled with a sense of sin and unworthiness and with fear that he does not care enough. Of the nine sections indicated in the title, by far the longest and most elaborate is the section devoted to the Son, about twenty-five hundred lines with the intricate rhyme scheme, A5BC2BC4AD5E2FF1E2D5. Faithful Teate called his second son "Nahum," meaning "comfort"; and, although the name was so unusual that "N. Tate" was often expanded by his contemporaries to "Nat" or "Nath" or even "Nathaniel" Tate,[5] the father's choice was appropriate both for his own avocation and for his son's vocation in that the Book of Nahum is one of the most poetic in the Bible.

I *Early Years*

Nahum, then, came from a family of Puritan ministers having many connections with Trinity College and, in the preceding generation, an interest in poetry. The first record we have of him is his registration, along with his brother Faithful, at Trinity College in June, 1668, when the brothers gave their place of birth as Dublin and the poet listed himself as sixteen years of age. It seems possible, however, that, since the father resided in England from about 1649 until after 1655, the recorded place of birth was merely nominal.[6] The brothers also stated that their previous training had been conducted by Henry Savage of Belfast, who had been at Trinity at the same time as their grandfather. Nahum seems to have had a poor opinion of his early training, for in 1684 he contrasted the education received by the students of his friend Lewis Maidwell with his own; he had been

> . . . by Pedants led astray,
> Who at my setting out mistook the way.
> With Terms confounded (such their Methods were)
> Those Rules my Cloud, that should have been my Star:
> Yet groping forwards through the Classicks went,
> Nor wholly of my Labors may repent:
> Strong holds, and hard to take, but in the sett,
> No Volume so obscure, no Author met
> So difficult, as William Lilly, yet.
> Without Geography led blindfold on,
> And ignorant when each exploit was done;
> Of wondrous Men, and wondrous Actions read,
> But all the while with Fairy Banquets fed.
> All hudled without knowing when, or where,
> Eutopian Fields, and Battels in the Air.[7]

Nahum and Faithful Tate entered Trinity as *pensionarii,* or as able to pay for their education; and as tutor they were assigned George Walker, who had also attended college with their grandfather and who, when he was promoted a few years later, was succeeded as Junior Fellow by the boys' uncle, Theophilus.[8] The curriculum was old-fashioned, and it is hardly surprising that a vigorous spirit like Swift should have been disgusted with it a decade later. Tate, however, seems to have found it tolerable: in his last year he was elected "scholar,"[9] and Trinity provided him with a background that gave him a reputation for learning among his contemporaries. He remembered the college with affection when, as poet laureate, he was invited to write the Ode for its centenary. Less than four years after the Battle of the Boyne, he viewed the college's future optimistically:

> Great Parent, hail! all hail to Thee,
> Who hast from last Distress surviv'd
> To see this joyful Year arriv'd
> Thy Muses second Jubilee.
>
> Another Century commencing
> No Decay in thee can trace;
> . . . .
> After War's Alarms repeated,
> And a Circling Age compleated,
> Vig'rous Off-spring thou dost raise.[10]

The Ode was sung to music written by Henry Purcell at the centennial observances on January 9, 1694.

The Dublin of Tate's youth was a comparatively large and rapidly growing city, its sixty thousand inhabitants making it the largest city after London in the British Isles.[11] And, under the leadership of Ormonde and his successors as lord-lieutenant, it rapidly became more Anglicized, especially more Londonized. Coffeehouses and bookstores multiplied rapidly after 1660; and the Smock Alley Theatre, as large as the Theatre Royal in Bridges Street and larger than Sir William Davenant's theater in Lincoln's-Inn-Fields, gave Dublin excellent drama and music. Although it was closed for about six months under Ormonde's Presbyterian successor, Baron Roberts, it was reopened in the spring of 1670, only to have the galleries collapse in December of that year at a performance of Ben Jonson's *Bartholomew Fair* —as stocks were being brought on stage for the Puritans, according to one account. The Puritans considered the event to be the judgment of a wrathful God.[12] If the second son of the late Faithful Teate, now in his third year at Trinity College, went to the theater, he would probably have been able to see some of the Shakespeare's plays, for at least fourteen of them, including *King Lear,* were in the Smock Alley repertory a few years later.[13]

II *In London under the Stuarts*

At some time between his graduation from Trinity College in 1672 and his first published poem in 1676, Tate arrived in London and made friends in literary circles. One of these friends was Thomas Flatman (1637-88), a popular poet in his own day and an accomplished painter of miniatures, whose *Poems and Songs,* which first appeared in 1674, was republished in 1676, 1682, and (with many additions) 1686.[14] The first edition was welcomed with congratulatory poems by six of Flatman's friends. Tate was not a member of this original group; but in the second edition the verses by Walter Pope were dropped, and their place was taken by Tate's first published poem, "To the Author on his Excellent Poems" by "N. Teat." Another set of congratulatory verses was by Charles Cotton, best known for his continuation of *The Compleat Angler.* Cotton also owned a copy of Tate's first book of verses, licensed in the same month that Flatman's volume was published, and handled by the same publisher.[15] This book, entitled simply *Poems,* and with the author's name spelled "Tate," contains sixty-nine short poems, many of them in the lugubrious vein of Flatman. The volume was dedicated to Dr. Walter Needham of Charterhouse (1631?-91?), who had been a classmate of Dryden both at Westminster School and at Trinity College, Cambridge, and was now a highly esteemed physician and, like Dryden, a member of the Royal Society.[16] Perhaps it was through Needham that Tate met Dryden, who was Tate's senior by twenty-one years and had been established for some time as the leading dramatist of his era.

In the next few years Tate followed Dryden's lead. He turned to the theater, and in the summer of 1678 his first play, *Brutus of Alba,* was performed at Dorset Garden.[17] In its modified heroics, simplicity of action, use of blank verse instead of rhyme, and selection of a Roman subject (Virgil's *Aeneid,* Book IV), the drama suggests the example of Dryden, whose *All for Love* had been performed at the end of the previous year. Tate's *Brutus of Alba* was licensed for publication on July 15 and was one of the first books to be published by Jacob Tonson, who later became the leading publisher of his time. The play was dedicated to Dryden's patron, the Earl of Dorset, whom the fledgling playwright addressed modestly by referring to himself as "the least of those that are blest with your Lordships Favour." For Tate's next play, *The Loyal General*, performed at Dorset Garden in the winter of 1679-80 and published early in 1680, Dryden wrote the Prologue. Meanwhile, Tate had translated three of Ovid's *Epistles* for the translation published by Tonson with a Preface by Dryden in 1680.

In 1682 Tate and Dryden collaborated again. Many years later, after Tate's death, Tonson published an account of what had happened: Dryden's *Absalom and Achitophel* being "applauded by everyone; and several persons pressing him to write a second part, he, upon declining it himself, spoke to Mr. Tate to write one, and gave his advice in the direction of it," as well as contributing the portraits of Og and Doeg and "some touches in other places."[18] *The Second Part of Absalom and Achitophel* was published in November. In the same year also, complimentary poems by Tate appeared in the third edition of *Absalom and Achitophel* and in Dryden's *The Medal*.

During these years Tate must have met many other literary friends of Dryden: the Earl of Mulgrave, Laurence Hyde, Sir George Etherege, the Earl of Roscommon, Thomas Southerne, Henry Dickinson (for whose translation of *A Critical History of the Old Testament* Tate wrote congratulatory verses), John Oldham (whose death in 1683 was lamented by Tate), Thomas Creech (for whose translation of Lucretius in 1683 Tate wrote commendatory verses), Nat Lee, and others.[19] His most important acquaintance about this time was Charles Sackville, Earl of Dorset and Middlesex (1643-1706), who was patron not only to Dryden and Tate but also to many others, including Thomas Shadwell, Thomas Durfey, Peter Motteux, and Matthew Prior; it was Dorset as lord chamberlain who recommended first Shadwell and then Tate as poets laureate. After leading a notoriously irresponsible life in his earlier years and after perhaps serving with Rochester as the original of Dorimant in Etherege's *Man of Mode,* Dorset settled down in the 1680's, opposed King James II in 1687-88, welcomed King William III, and served as lord chamberlain and as a member of the Privy Council before he retired in 1697, when he was accused of having "overtaxed the spoils system."[20]

Although it might seem from Dorset's early life and his amatory verses that he would have little in common with the son of Faithful Teate, his taste was broad enough for him to admire *Paradise Lost* and to own a portrait of Milton. In addition to receiving the dedication of Tate's first play, Dorset was complimented by Tate in his *Poem on the Late Promotion of Several Eminent Persons* (1694), and Tate wrote an elegy on the death of Dorset's second wife. The poet also dedicated his edition of Sir John Davies's *Original, Nature, and Immortality of the Soul* (1697) to Dorset, saying that the latter had shown it to him; this work, frequently republished in the seventeenth and eighteenth centuries, was often employed in current religious controversies about the immortality of the soul.[21]

Meanwhile, Tate was attempting to succeed in the theater by making Shakespeare relevant. Shadwell had already commented on social and political affairs in an adaptation of Shakespeare's *Timon of Athens* that had appeared in January, 1679;[22] and Dryden had also reflected on the political situation—especially the lack of respect for authority—in his adaptation a few months later of *Troilus and Cressida*. Although Tate began by revising *King Lear* (on the advice, he said, of his friend Thomas Boteler, to whom he dedicated the play), his adaptation of *Richard II* was probably acted first.[23] In these years, when the exclusion of a successor to the throne was being considered by Parliament, the deposition of an English king was a dangerous topic; and *Richard II* was forbidden twice, once in December and once in January. On the second occasion the play was performed under a title that seemed to place the action in Sicily ("The Sicilian Usurper"), and some changes were made in the names of characters—an attempt either to deceive the censor or to remove the cause of his objections. On at least one occasion, too, the play was stopped after the second performance.[24] The playwright normally received the profits of the third night, and Tate was disappointed; when he published the adaptation, he included a long, grieving

Preface, protesting that the play was not disloyal and had not even been read by those who condemned it. Since a "corrected & amended version" was licensed on March 18, 1682,[25] it seems likely that Tate's complaint resulted in a reconsideration, although there is no record of further performances.

Tate's *History of King Lear* with its famous happy ending was performed by the Duke's Company, with Thomas Betterton as Lear and with Elizabeth Barry as Cordelia. Although this play shows the maltreatment and attempted deposition of a king, the authorities evidently did not find it dangerous. In his Prologue, Tate was pointedly political; referring to the moral value of his adaptation, he observed:

> Poets must take the churches Teaching Trade,
> Since Priests their Province of Intrigue invade;
> But we the worst in this Exchange have got,
> In vain our Poets Preach, whilst Church-men Plot.

By the end of the year, Tate had another and frankly political adaptation ready: *The Ingratitude of a Common-Wealth*, based on *Coriolanus* with (as the title suggests) emphasis placed upon the irresponsibility of the crowd. It was acted—probably several times, including a performance before the Moroccan ambassador on January 14, 1682—but it does not seem to have endured beyond its first season.

After the Shakespeare adaptations of 1680-81 and the work with Dryden in satire and translation in 1680-82, the year 1683 was comparatively quiet for Tate. But in 1684-85 he produced a variety of literary wares: a much revised and enlarged edition of his *Poems* was advertised in May, 1684, and was followed by a collection, *Poems by Several Hands and on Several Occasions Collected by N. Tate*, which contained the work of a number of poets including the editor but, according to a note to the reader, nothing that could "give offence to the chastest Ear." Tate was also honored by being invited to write the Saint Cecilia's Day Ode for 1685. He had two new plays ready as well: one was the durable farce *A Duke and No Duke*, based upon Aston Cokain's *Trappolin Suppos'd a Prince*, and the other was an unsuccessful comedy, *Cuckolds-Haven*, adapted from Ben Jonson, George Chapman, and John Marston's *Eastward Ho!* When King Charles died on February 6, 1685, Tate was quickly ready with an elegy—even more quickly than Dryden, apparently, whose *Threnodia Augustalis* was published early in March,[26] for Tate in his poem calls on "Asaph" (his name for Dryden in *The Second Part of Absalom and Achitophel*) to sing. In November, 1685, *The Term Catalogues* advertised a new translation of the *Aethiopian History* of Heliodorus, to which Tate contributed one hundred and sixty pages.[27] The observation of Tate's contemporaries that he was a "slow" writer does not seem applicable to this portion of his career.

Tate had praised James II highly in *The Second Part of Absalom and Achitophel* and in the first selection in his *Poems* of 1684, and he continued his praise in the elegy on Charles II. The new king was complimented on his Valor, his Justice, and "all the Mercies of the Stuart's Line":

> Blest Prince! by Heav'n and Charles Example led!
> So may His Honours double on Your Head.
> The long-liv'd Heir of all His Blessings prove,
> On Earth succeeding to His Subjects Love,
> And to the same kind Angels Care Above.[28]

Although Tate's hope seems ironic in the light of later events, it was the dominant attitude of the time. It was probably genuine on Tate's part as well, even in view of his enthusiastic support of William III a few years later; for times and men's attitudes changed rapidly in the seventeenth century. A reasonable, patriotic man of principle might well support Oliver Cromwell in the 1650's, Charles II in the 1660's and 1670's, James II in the middle 1680's, and William III after 1687. Indeed, the country as a whole did so, for each ruler seemed to bring the order and stability needed at the time. Nevertheless, Tate's enthusiasm, like the nation's, could not have extended to James's religion; and Tate must have been increasingly dismayed by the King's intolerance and tactlessness during the next few years. In spite of the success of Tate's *A Duke and No Duke* and his adaptation of John Fletcher's *Island Princess,* which was performed at court in 1687, Tate seems to have turned away from the stage to translations, editions, and compilations, including his translation of Girolamo Fracastolo's account of the history and cure of syphilis (1686).

It is evident from Tate's dedications that he was trying to find patrons among influential persons at court, and perhaps it was at this time that Edward Howard, second Earl of Carlisle, helped him.[29] *The Island Princess* was dedicated to the Earl of Mulgrave, King James's comptroller; and Sir George Hewitt, who has been proposed as the original of Etherege's Sir Foppling Flutter, received the dedication of *A Duke and No Duke*.[30] *Cuckolds-Haven* was dedicated to Edmund Ashton, a friend of Shadwell's who was an officer in the king's Life Guards and a member of James's Parliament, but who was to lose his offices under William.[31] In the dedication, Tate shared Ashton's regret over the recent death of their mutual friend, the Earl of Roscommon: "of many Obligations that endear his Memory to me, the Opportunity of your Acquaintance was not the least; while I have heard you discant together on your beloved Authours, Time seem'd to me to be revolv'd, and I thought myself in the Court of Augustus." Roscommon had presided over an "Academy" for the study and refinement of the English language. It had included Dorset and Dryden among its members,[32] and Tate was probably associated with this group as well. By this time, too, he numbered musicians among his acquaintances, the most notable being John Playford, the leading music publisher of the day, whose death he lamented in 1687; Henry Purcell, with whom he was soon to collaborate in *Dido and Aeneas*; and Purcell's mentor John Blow, Master of the Children of the Chapel Royal and Purcell's predecessor and successor as organist at Westminster Abbey.

Although Tate is not known to have had any occupation other than writing, it has been suggested that he may have been a schoolmaster for a time between 1687 and 1692.[33] The strongest evidence in support of this suggestion is an announcement in *The Gentleman's Journal* in 1692 of "a most useful Treatise" by Tate which, though "not yet publish'd, . . . may well bear the Name of, *The Compleat Tutor*": it is to discuss the value of instruction, the choice of a good teacher, methods of teaching, Classical authors, and "Rules . . . to attain to the Writing of a good English Style."[34] Unfortunately, this work seems not to have been published. The fact that Tate's output was thinner during these years than before or after might have been a consequence of his taking up another means of making his living; and his most notable work at this time—the libretto for *Dido and Aeneas*—was written for schoolgirls.

Tate's long friendship with his close contemporary Lewis Maidwell (1650-1715) also suggests that he may have done some formal teaching. Maidwell was the head of a school in Westminster; he dabbled in the theater, wrote a historical account of Horace's life, and from 1700 to 1705 pestered Parliament with a new scheme for a public academy, which he described in his *Essay upon the Necessity and Excellency of Education* in 1705.[35] His *Nova Gramatices Experimenta: or, Some New Essays of a Natural and Artificial Grammar* was not published until 1707, when it appeared "with a Paraenetic Poem by Mr. Tate"; but twenty-three years earlier, in the 1684 *Poems*, Tate had praised Maidwell both in his "On the Translation of Eutropius" and in "To Mr. Maidwell on his New Grammar." In the latter he praised Maidwell's scheme on the pedagogical grounds that, "So short and clear all thy Instructions lie, / They teach the Mind, not load the Memory".[36] In 1706, too, Tate published a "paraphrase" in English of some Latin poems of Maidwell's on "the Glories of Great Britain" prefaced with praise of the "Signal Services" his "Worthy Friend" "has done his Country in the Happy Education of many Persons of Quality."[37]

III *William and Mary*

Since Tate had praised James II highly in 1685 and before, he was thought of as belonging with Settle, Durfey, and Dryden among the Tory poets at the time of the Revolution of 1688.[38] Nevertheless, William of Orange and Mary, reserved, conservatively Protestant, and inclined to encourage a higher standard of public morality, were a royal couple whom Tate could celebrate with genuine enthusiasm. Nine months after they were proclaimed king and queen, he sounded the note he was to continue throughout William's reign:

> Saturnian Days revolve, of former Crimes,
> If any Seeds molest our Halcyon Times,
> And Rouze our Mars, on him lies all the Care,

Defence and Freedom nere were bought too Dear.
He only Arms to make our Dangers cease,
His Wars are Glorious, for his End is Peace.
The Muses once were Sacred, give 'em leave,
One Vote for Britain's Welfare to conceive;
They Sum Their Wishes up, in one short Pray'r,
(Join all True Hearts) Long Live the Royal Pair.[39]

This tribute was made in November, 1689; in *The Term Catalogues* for the following February was advertised *A Pastoral Dialogue,* published anonymously in 1690 and 1691, and then acknowledged by Tate and printed with the title *A Poem Occasioned by the Late Discontents . . . With Reflections Upon the Rise and Progress of Priestcraft.*[40] This poem was followed by a sequel entitled *A Poem, Occasioned by His Majesty's Voyage to Holland,* in which the shepherd Philander dreams that he is in the Elysian Fields, where he encounters the shades of Abraham Cowley, Milton, and Edmund Waller. Milton, who has stopped praising commonwealths and now praises William instead, is engaged in attempting to "justify Suspected Providence" for the wound William received at the Battle of the Boyne. Tate also flattered the king in the dedicatory epistle (addressed to the queen) of a translation of Quintus Curtius's *Life of Alexander the Great,* advertised in November 1690:[41] William is found to resemble Alexander.

The Preface that accompanied *A Pastoral Dialogue* and *A Poem Occasioned by the Late Discontents* is interesting both for its forceful expression of Tate's views of the political situation and for its imitation of the noble style and grave tone of Milton's prose writings, especially *Areopagitica* (the poem itself echoes "Lycidas"):[42]

> I Could heartily have wish'd there had been no Occasion offer'd, or Subject-matter for an Essay of this kind. After so happy and wonderful a Revolution as we have seen, when our Hopes were grown desperate, and our Liberty reduc'd to its very last gasp, to have the only Remedy in Nature so effectually apply'd, so miraculous a Recovery perform'd; after all this, to find English-men, and such as pretend to no other Interest or Religion but That of their Country; to find Them

> expressing Dissatisfaction, everywhere busie in sowing Dissention, obstructing, as far as in them lies, the Progress of Affairs, and unhinging the present Settlement (upon which alone depends the Safety of these Nations, and common Quiet of Europe); This is so just a Cause of Indignation, as must make every Lover of his Countrey to turn Satyrist, or, at least, excuse the honest Zeal of such as upon this Occasion express their Resentments. . . .
>
> The Unreasonableness (that is to say, the Impossibility) of Force in matters of meer Conscience and Opinion, has demonstrated it self through all Ages. Our Dissenters have had their Faults, and they have suffer'd: Neither is it the least Blessing amongst those Great and Many that seem to be reserv'd for His present Majesty's Reign, That we do not yet despair of a Comprehension. His Majesty has, with more than Constantine's Piety, signaliz'd His Royal Inclination; the ablest of our Spiritual Guides are zealous Endeavourers for it: and That (amongst other weighty Reasons) for the True Interest and Inviolable Security of the Church Establish'd: Which, as it influences the Publick Happiness, it is the Duty of ev'n the meanest Lay-man to be sollicitous for it.[43]

It is hard to believe that a man who writes in this manner is not sincere, and it is easy to believe that he would make a useful poet laureate. Shadwell died on November 19, 1692, and three days later Narcissus Luttrell recorded the rumor that Tate would be the next laureate; the appointment was made on December 8, when Tate received the laureateship at a salary of one hundred pounds with the traditional butt of canary wine at Christmas. At the same time Thomas Rymer was made historiographer royal at the higher salary of two hundred pounds.[44] Peter Motteux greeted the "universally pleasing" news of the appointments of Tate and Rymer in his *Gentleman's Journal*: "You and all the ingenious are so well acquainted with their worth, that I dare not dwell on its praise here, lest by faint expressions I wrong the bright Idea's which all that have a sence of the Politer Studies must have of these two Gentlemens Merits."[45]

It is not entirely clear why Tate received one hundred pounds while Rymer was given two hundred pounds. Dryden had received two hundred pounds as both laureate and historiographer and, beginning in 1677, an additional one hundred pounds. It was made explicit in his reappointment by James in 1685 that the extra one hundred pounds was "for his encouragement diligently to attend the said employment"—presumably in both offices.[46] Shadwell also had received three hundred pounds for the two positions. Yet Tate was appointed "Poet Laureat, with all the rights, profits etc. as amply as" Chaucer, Ben Jonson, Davenant, Dryden, or Shadwell "with the annuity or yearly pension of £100. . . ."[47] When in 1700 Tate asked for an additional two hundred pounds a year, complaining that "his salary of poet laureate [was] but £100 *per ann.*, of £300 which his predecessors enjoyed," the government compromised by giving him a single grant of two hundred pounds but added nothing to his salary.[48] On the other hand, Rymer would have felt slighted if he had received less than two hundred pounds, for the only other man to hold the historiographer's office alone since the Restoration—James Howell—had received two hundred pounds during his tenure, 1661-66.[49] Although Rymer and Tate each had grounds for claiming more than one hundred pounds, Rymer had a claim for the specific sum of two hundred pounds; and he may have pressed for his rights more vigorously than Tate.

The duties of the laureateship were not clearly defined. The earlier court poets of the seventeenth century, Jonson and Davenant, had contributed masques frequently, but Dryden and Shadwell had not continued the tradition. After his appointment as laureate, Dryden had written political satires, philosophical and religious poems, and panegyrics such as *Threnodia Augustalis* and *Britannia Rediviva;* but Shadwell's laureate verse consisted of only a few odes. Tate, however, was more self-conscious and explicit about his duties. Not only did he write a number of birthday and New Year odes, but he also asserted again and again that it was the poet's responsibility—especially the laureate's responsibility—to promote religion and morality. As he stated in 1706, "Poets have always reckon'd it, next their Tribute to the Temple, and Hymns of Divine Praise, the Greatest Branch of their Charter to Celebrate the Worthies of their Time and Country."[50] Such aims harmonized with the reforming spirit of the times and with the increasing tendency to look for a practical purpose in literature. A decade later, when Tate was reappointed to the laureateship under Queen Anne, he was praised for his "good Learning, Strict Morals, and . . . singular Modesty" and because "he is even endeavouring to reform the Stage."[51]

The appointment as laureate resulted in new literary activity by Tate. He was ready with an *Ode upon the New-Year* and odes on the birthdays of Queen Mary (April 30) and King William (November 4). His five-hundred-page translation of Pierre Coste's work, *The Life of Lewis of Bourbon,* was published early in 1693, and *A Present for the Ladies: Being an Historical Vindication of the Female Sex. To which is added, The Character of an Accomplish'd Virgin, Wife, and Widow, in Verse* was designed to appeal to the increasingly important feminine public: the first edition in 1692 was succeeded by a second in the following year. In this work a 12-page Preface defends ladies from charges of inconstancy, pride, and secrecy; then 101 pages of prose offer examples of female virtue and 22 pages of "characters" follow in heroic couplets. A new edition of *A Duke and no Duke* with a much-expanded Preface defending farce was ready by May, 1693; and a second edition of the translation of Fracastoro's *Syphilis* was also published.

Shorter pieces were appearing elsewhere: translations of two of Juvenal's *Satires;*[52] an epistle in the first edition of the Earl of Orrery's farce *Guzman;* two poems in *Harmonia Sacra;* a brief complimentary poem in *A History of the Athenian Society;* and several poems in *The Gentleman's Journal.* In January, 1694, the Dublin ode was performed; and before the end of the year, Tate had edited Ogier Ghislain de Busbeq's *Epistles* and published his *Poem on the Late Promotion* as well as an elegy on Joseph Washington and an ode on the king's birthday. When Archbishop Tillotson died on November 22 and Queen Mary on December 28, Tate was ready within a few weeks with substantial elegies on both.

Tate's activity is the more impressive because it was at this time that he was completing, in collaboration with Nicholas

Brady, one of his most ambitious and successful projects, *A New Version of the Psalms of David.* The full one hundred and fifty Psalms were published in 1696, but the roots of this undertaking go back as far as the *Poems* of 1677, in which Tate included three verses of Psalm 46. There was much revision of the Psalms in 1698, and a *Supplement* with other "hymns" appeared in 1700. The first complete edition of the *New Version,* dedicated to King William, was quickly "Allowed and Permitted to be used in all such Churches . . . as shall think fit to receive the same." In the same year that the Psalms first appeared, Tate also published an anthology of religious verse, *Miscellanea Sacra,* with an eight-page Preface about verse on "Divine and Moral Subjects." The collection contained poems by a number of writers, including the editor; and it was sufficiently popular to be republished twice during the next decade.

Tate also attempted to help in the reformation of the theater. Jeremy Collier, whom Tate might have encountered at Knole when Collier held a living there from 1677 to 1679,[53] published his *Short View of the Immorality and Profaneness of the English Stage* in March, 1698. To the storm of printed material that followed Collier's attack, Tate contributed nothing; but less than a year later he did send a proposal to either the Bishop of London or the Archbishop of Canterbury "for Regulating of the Stage & Stage-Plays."[54] His suggestions are interesting: "First, That Supervisors of Plays be appointed by the Government"; second, that all plays—old and new—be altered and reformed, by their authors if they are living and otherwise by others; third, that "Encouragement" (presumably, financial) be provided the revisers and that penalties accompany their default; and fourth, that no gentlemen be permitted backstage and no women be allowed to wear vizard masks to the theater. He concludes with the observation that it is "Absolutely Necessary" that the stage be "Reform'd or Silence'd." Tate's letter, dated February 6, preceded by twelve days the king's order that the stage be reformed.

Tate himself made two other efforts to participate in reformation of the theater. The first was a contribution to Cavendish

Weedon's musical entertainment for the members of Parliament in Stationers' Hall on January 31, 1702. In his dedication, Weedon congratulated both houses of Parliament on their "Generous Concurrence" with the king in "his Extraordinary Zeal for the Promoting of Religion and Piety," pointing out the valuable contribution that could be made by "Divine Musick; by which the Minds of People are sweetly surpriz'd into Pious Ardour, and Charm'd into Devotion by Delight."[55] Tate's contributions are an opening poem on the decline of music from its sacred function in earlier times "To Serenades, Masques, Banquets, Rev'ling Rage; / Buffoon'ry, Farce; those Witch-Crafts of the Stage, / And dire Diversions of a Graceless Age" to its even lower state of serving for "thoughtless Madrigals of Lisping Beaus." After an interruption for "a Mournful Symphony," music is revived for the present occasion. Psalm 19 was then sung to music composed by William Turner, followed by a brief Oration and then Psalm 96 set to music by Blow. The entertainment concluded with another poem by Tate in praise of music, king, and Parliament, and with Psalm 21 with music by Turner. Tate's other effort to participate in a reformed theater was a sentimentalized and verbally trimmed adaptation of John Webster's *White Devil,* which he made between 1702 and 1707. Never performed, it was well enough known to be quoted several times in the mock-critical annotations of Henry Fielding's *The Tragedy of Tragedies* (1731).

After Tate's appointment as laureate, he usually avoided controversy and controversial subjects as much as he could; but two exceptions are worthy of note. The first began with Sir Richard Blackmore's *Satyr against Wit* (November, 1699), in which Tate was included with Dryden and the wits of Will's Coffee House. Blackmore said: "T[ate] will subscribe, but set no Payment-Day, / For his slow Muse you must with Patience stay, / He's honest, and as Wit comes in, will pay."[56] Tate alluded to Blackmore in the Postscript to *Panacea: A Poem Upon Tea* (1700), where he replied briefly to several of his critics and then apologized for "this Trifling, 'tis paying Nonsense in its own Coin." He continued: "In good Earnest, 'tis high time for the Fraternity to return to their Senses; they have so long

Ridicul'd One Another, till the Men, that had some Wit, are become Diversion for them that have None." Meanwhile, someone else, probably Nicholas Brady, defended Tate in *Commendatory Verses* (advertised in March), remarking that the Exchequer and "half the Lords" are no faster to pay than Tate and concluding: "Then be advis'd; Rail not at Tate so fast, / A Psalm of his may chance to be thy last."

A reply, addressed to Brady in *Discommendatory Verses* (advertised in April), pointed out that at least Tate was "Honest" and paid when he could—which was more than could be said for Brady (who seems to have had difficulty living within his income).[57] It must have amused contemporaries to see the king's physician (Blackmore) quarreling with the king's chaplain (Brady) over the king's poet laureate; certainly Tate came out of the affair with more dignity than anyone else. All parties seem agreed about his honesty but, rather puzzlingly, they all seem agreed about his slowness. Three possible explanations are, first, that "slow" was intended in the sense of dull or stupid (but Blackmore seems to have intended the sense of taking a long time to perform an act); second, that he had a reputation for working long hours to produce as much as he did; and, third, that his slowness in speech and action in public may have been transferred unjustifiably to his literary activity.

The other controversy was more significant, and Tate played a more active role. This was the Kentish Petition in 1701. The king's conflict with Parliament had reached a climax, and Parliament had failed to act on urgent matters of foreign policy; instead, its time was spent in bickering and in attacking the king's ministers. In February, Tate had welcomed the members hopefully with *A Congratulatory Poem on the New Parliament Assembled on This Great Conjuncture of Affairs*, in which the four goddesses—Britannia, Batavia, Eusebia, and Europa—urged the members to act to save Europe. A second edition of Tate's poem was advertised in May. Early in the same month, disgusted with Parliament's failure to act, the Quarter Sessions of the County of Kent delivered a petition to the House, presented by five leading citizens. When the five were arrested, the more vigorously worded *Legion's Memorial to the House of Commons* was presented by its author Daniel Defoe in person; and shortly thereafter the original petitioners were released amid rejoicing.[58] Tate wrote a brief poem of seventy-seven lines entitled *The Kentish Worthies,* in which the petitioners' actions are declared worthy of celebration by Spenser, Milton, and Waller, and in which the Muses rival each other to greet them. This poem produced the only substantial personal attack on Tate, a poem by "Andrew Dothat," entitled *A Satyr on the Kentish-Men and T—–te, the Poet.* Tate is accused of being opposed to Parliament because he resents its lack of enthusiasm for his Psalms. Dothat's diction, imagination, and versification are atrocious: Tate is a "Poor, softly, factious Tool"; and the writer hopes that Tate's "Bays" may become ". . . a Cherry-Tree, / And none out of poor Kent-Land may him see." The last line, which is the last in the poem, gives a fair impression of Dothat's success in writing pentameters.

IV *Queen Anne*

Tate was fifty when Anne became queen in 1702, and the considerable drop in his productivity thereafter suggests that, whether or not he had been in poor health earlier, he was not well then. He did some translating of Ovid and Lucian during his last fourteen years,[59] but otherwise he produced an average of one official poem per year, a prose defense of the *New Version of the Psalms* in 1710, an adaptation of Webster's *White Devil,* and little else. He seems to have needed the money that additional literary labors could have brought him. Apparently he had never married; and, although his salary of one hundred pounds might have been adequate for a cautious, elderly bachelor at a time when shopkeepers and tradesmen received about forty-five pounds per year, clergymen fifty pounds to seventy-two pounds, and persons in liberal arts and sciences about sixty pounds,[60] Tate's stipend was not always paid. There is no record of his having to petition during William's reign in order to collect his back salary, though Rymer had to petition several times for his. However, Tate's request in 1700 for an increase in his salary to three hundred pounds included the plea that he needed help in his "useful" undertaking of the Psalms. Under Queen Anne, he was granted an extra thirty pounds per year in lieu of his butt of canary wine; and, although he received additional assistance with the Psalms, he also had to ask for his back salary.[61] In 1696, he had signed a joint contract with Brady and the Stationers Company, dividing the profits of the *New Version* into equal shares; but apparently this arrangement did not endure.[62] During Tate's later years he seems to have been in danger from his creditors. Two years before his death he made a bitter contribution to a volume entitled *Memoirs of the Mint and Queen's-Bench.* Likening himself to Ovid banished from Rome, Tate addressed the marshal, his "second Patron":

> Take Courage Bard, once more our Joys are crown'd,
> We have a second Patron here, a second Dorset found.
> The first to Thee, Great Britain's Lawrel gave,
> But THIS Releasement from a Living Grave.
> When for Church-Service to Confinement run,
> And Wretchedly, yet Gloriously undone,
> O therefore to your silent Cell retire,
> To sing him Thanks, then break your Luckless Lyre.[63]

Evidently, Tate had been imprisoned for debt; "Church-Service" is presumably his financially unprofitable religious writings, including the Psalms.

The laureate or panegyrical verse that Tate wrote during these years celebrates some of the major events of Queen Anne's reign: *The Triumph, or Warriours Welcome* (1705) glories in the victory of Blenheim; *The Triumph of Union* (1707) celebrates the long-awaited union of Scotland and England; and *The Triumph of Peace* (1713) welcomes the Treaty of Utrecht. The queen was praised in *Portrait-Royal* (1703), which described John Closterman's portrait of her; in *Britannia's Prayer for the Queen* (1706); in *A Congratulatory Poem on Her Majesties Happy Recovery,* when Anne recovered sufficiently from an illness to attend the opening of Parliament in March, 1714; and in the elegy *A Poem Sacred to . . .* Queen *Anne,* published posthumously in 1716. The prince consort had a poem to himself in *A Congratulatory Poem to His Royal Highness Prince George of Denmark* (1707), which was frugally republished as *The Muse's Memorial of His Royal Highness* after George's death in October, 1708. In *The Muse's Memorial, Of the . . . Earl of Oxford* (1712), Tate rejoiced in Harley's triumph over the Whigs in Parliament; and in *The Muse's Bower, An Epithalamium* (1713), he celebrated the marriage of Harley's daughter Elizabeth. In addition to the support of the Earl of Oxford, Tate seems to have attempted around 1706 to obtain that of Charles Howard, third Earl of Carlisle and son of his former patron, and, near the end of Tate's life, that of the Duke of Buckingham.[64]

One other effort of Tate's during his closing years is of special interest because it is a periodical nearly contemporary with *The Spectator* of Addison and Steele. In 1713 the sixty-one-year-old laureate joined with "M. Smith," the author of *Memoirs of the Mint* and of a long religious poem *The Vision*, in issuing *The Monitor*, "Intended for the Promoting of Religion and Virtue, and Suppressing of Vice and Immorality." Beginning with the issue of March 2, it appeared three times a week for several weeks and then twice a week until it expired with the twenty-first number (April 20-24). Each issue was a single sheet containing from one to five poems on religious and moral subjects.

The story of this publication's rise and fall is told by the brief editorial comments that conclude each issue. In Number 1, it was announced that the first three issues would be given away free; in Number 3, subscribers were told that their papers would be delivered; in Number 5, the papers were being sent to charity schools, where the children would learn the poems by heart; in Number 11, subscribers were told that they need pay nothing at all until they had received six issues. In Number 16, the number of issues was to be cut back from three to two a week because "one Day in a Week must be appropriated to the Entring the Subscribers Names in the Books, and the adjusting all Accounts"; but three issues later, the editors confessed "that the Town in General, and also they who particularly approve of our Divine Poems, seem desirous of having other Entertaining Subjects mixt with them," and therefore *The Monitor* would make way for *The Oracle*, to be published by others. Number 20 urged subscribers to pay whatever was due when the next and last issue was delivered. Number 17 is of particular interest because it tells for the first time in print the story of Dryden's visiting Milton to ask permission to convert *Paradise Lost* into a rhymed drama, with Milton's reply that Dryden might "Tagg [his] lines" if he wished.[65]

Smith complained that he had lost money on the project, and doubtless Tate had as well. After the periodical had expired, the sets that remained were bound together and sent "to People of the best Character," and this experiment proved so successful that Smith republished in book form the forty-one poems in *The Monitor*, at least eight of which were by Tate, along with a very distinguished subscription list.[66] In this second edition the preliminary material was by Smith, though the "Poet-Laureat" was referred to as one of the original editors; it seems likely, therefore, that Tate had nothing to do with this edition but that it was published before his death (before "Poet-Laureat" would refer to someone else.) Presumably, Tate received none of the profits.

On July 30, 1715, Tate died in the Mint. His burial is recorded under the date August 1—exactly a year after Queen Anne died—in the register of Saint George's Church, Southwark ("Little Dorrit's Church"): "Nahum Tate, next to Prince Eugene the Mint."[67] In less than two weeks the court had announced his successor, Nicholas Rowe.[68] Tate's death was apparently not unexpected; for, when the elegy on Queen Anne was published in the following year, readers were informed that "the Gentleman who had this Poem (among the other Manuscript-Copies of the late Mr. Tate) in his Custody on Account of a Friendship long contracted between them" had reported that the poem was not published during the poet's lifetime because he had determined to give up writing verse after this elegy, and his friends urged him not to publish an elegy on one monarch unless he was willing to welcome the next.[69] The story is not quite true, for Tate did write a brief "Song on His Majesty's Birth-Day, May 28, 1715," published in the *Flying Post* for June 9-11; but the elegy on Anne apparently was his last substantial poem. We may take as biographical, then, the concluding couplet:

While I, to solemn Shades, depriv'd of Day,
Retire, and Mourn the short Remains of Life away.

CHAPTER 3

Short Poems and Translations of Ovid and Juvenal

OF THE SIXTY-NINE PIECES in the first edition of Tate's *Poems* (1677), about half belong to the tradition of melancholy verse that reaches back to the early years of the seventeenth century and forward to the period of Tate's laureateship around 1700, a time whose "widespread fondness for melancholy subjects in literature" and for funeral elegies has been emphasized by Amy Reed and by J. W. Draper.[1] The publication of Robert Burton's *Anatomy of Melancholy* in an eighth edition the year before Tate's poems appeared testifies to the continuing interest in the subject. However, the most respectable and most talented writer of this kind of verse during the 1670's was Tate's friend Flatman, who wrote of death so often that, when he composed an elegy on his brother, he could begin with the thought that he had nothing on the subject left to say.[2] Tate commented on Flatman's common theme in his first published poem from the point of view of the admiring apprentice:

> Strange Magick of thy Wit and Stile,
> Which to their Griefs Mankind can reconcile!
> While thy Philander's tuneful Voice we hear,
> Condoling our disastrous State,
> Toucht with a sense of our hard Fate,
> We sigh perhaps, or drop a Tear;
> But he the mournful Song so sweetly sings,
> That more of Pleasure than Regret it brings, . . .[3]

In another poem, "Ode. To my Ingenious Friend, Mr. Flatman," Tate emphasized his apprenticeship as Icarus to Flatman's Daedalus.[4]

Especially interesting are the melancholy poems which seem to look forward to the eighteenth century or beyond. Tate's "Mid-Night Thought," for example, seems to anticipate Edward Young's *Night Thoughts* (1742), two-thirds of a century later:

Now that the twinkling Stars essay
A faint Resemblance of the Day,
Shewn fairer now for being set
In Night (like Diamonds in Jett)
Let me (repos'd within this Grove)
The solemn Season once improve.
Restless, Alass! from Sun to Sun,
A Round of Business I have run:
Whilst others slept, projecting lay,
My Night as thoughtful as my Day;
. . . .
How long since I did meditate
Of Life, of Death, and future State?
Approaching Fate his Pace will keep,
Let Mortals watch, or let them sleep.
What Sound is that?—a Passing Bell!
Then to Eternity farewell! . . .[5]

And in "Disappointed" Tate seems to anticipate the mood of Matthew Arnold:

From Clime to Clime with restless Toyl we Roam,
But sadly still our old Griefs we retain,
And with us bear beyond the spacious Main
The same unquiet selves we brought from Home.[6]

Tate's melancholy is not the "divinest Melancholy" that Milton hails in "Il Penseroso," but rather the Burtonian disease which, in "Melancholy," Tate calls the "Malignant Humour, Poyson to my Blood," from which he wants to escape.[7] Usually, his melancholy poems have a strong moral emphasis. "On a Diseased Old Man, Who Wept at thought of leaving the World," for example, and "Disswasion of an Aged Friend from leaving His Retirement" argue—one harshly, the other gently—the worthlessness of mundane concerns.

The longest poem in the 1677 volume, "The Vision. Written in a dangerous Fit of Sickness," is of this kind. Dreaming that he enters "Death's sad Courts," the poet comes to a cave filled with tablets hung on threads, each giving the story of a life. He finds one with his name on it and learns that he is about to die. When Death enters with his dart, scepter, skull, bloody attendants, and assistant diseases, the Dreamer pleads for his life on the grounds that, though he has been sinful, he should be allowed time to repent. His plea is denied, but, as the Demons are about to seize him, his Guardian Angel disperses them. Observing that the Dreamer is indeed close to death, the Angel gives him a vision of his own body, which the Dreamer addresses with disgust and loathing. Momentarily, he is given a vision of Heaven, and then he awakens to life—which seems to be Hell.[8]

The moral emphasis appears also in his "On the Present Corrupted State of Poetry" in the 1677 volume:

> Write thy own Elegy Apostate Art,
> Thou Angel once of Light;
> But, since thy Fall, a Friend of Night,
> Mankind endeav'ring to pervert.

The poet contrasts the noble religious origins of poetry, the support it has received from wise and potent kings, its dignity in more virtuous ages when it was used "t'embalm some Worthy Name," and its freedom from mercenary concerns in the past with its present tendency to encourage "The Vanity and Vices of the Age; / Flatt'ring in Courts, and Rev'lling on the Stage."[9] He laments the poverty that befalls "Th'Unfortunate Man, whom any Muse befriends."

I *Other Models*

The 1677 *Poems* was a typical first effort in that it contained many experiments and imitations of various recent or contemporary writers. One of these was Milton, who had died only three years earlier. As Raymond D. Havens has pointed out, Tate's poem "On Snow fall'n in Autumn, and Dissolv'd by the Sun" is an imitation of two stanzas of Milton's *Nativity* Ode.[10]

"Lycidas," from which Tate also borrowed in *A Pastoral Dialogue* (1691), is echoed at the end of "Melancholy," in which Tate answers his own questionings of the "Book of Fate" as follows:

> Who seeks for Happiness with nicest Care
> Must watch its Seasons, and frequent its Haunt.
> Delight is a rich tender Plant
> That Springs not in all Soils, and all the Year:[11]

Phoebus had replied similarly to the poet's question in "Lycidas" (ll. 78-80): "Fame is no plant that grows on mortal soil, / Nor in the glistering foil / Set off to th'world, . . ."

Later, Tate expressed his admiration for Milton's style and occasionally even imitated it. Although he seems never to have published a poem in blank verse, he referred in 1688 to the "Majestic Plainness" of Milton's style, "just" but "Subservient to the Thought."[12] In his epigram "On the Spectator," published at the end of an essay by Addison in *The Spectator* for September 19, 1712 (No. 488), Tate imitates Milton's manner:

> When first the *Tatler* to a Mute was turn'd,
> Great Britain for her Censor's Silence mourn'd.
> Robb'd of his sprightly Beams she wept the Night,
> Till the *Spectator* rose, and blaz'd as bright.
> So the first Man the Sun's first Setting view'd,
> And sigh'd, 'till circling Day his Joys renew'd;
> Yet doubtful how that second Sun to name,
> Whether a bright Successor, or the same.
> So we: but now from this Suspence are freed,
> Since all agree, who both with Judgment read,
> 'Tis the same sun, and does himself succeed.

The Miltonic effect of the four-line metaphor describing the "first Man" is conveyed principally by the phrase "circling Day" and by the omissions of both subjects and verbs in lines 7 and 8 and of the verb in line 9. It seems surprising that Tate did not imitate Milton more than he did, for he seems to have regarded his predecessor as England's greatest poet; and, as the son of a Puritan minister, as a man with some scholarly attainments and an interest in education, and as a supporter of the poet's important role in encouraging moral reform, Tate must have found much of Milton's thought and attitude congenial. In part, the explanation of Tate's independence of Miltonic influence probably lies in the very different kinds of poems the two men were called upon to write.

About one-third of the poems in Tate's 1677 collection are love lyrics. Most are short and are set in a pastoral background in which shepherds—usually anonymous but sometimes named Strephon, Thirsis, Alexis, or Damon—discourse with or about shepherdesses, Laura, Sylvia, Larissa, Fanarett, Olinda, or Julia. Love is generally painful for Tate's shepherds. In "The Escape," in fact, the lady fisherman hooks her lover; but, in her eagerness to land her catch, she lets him escape with a permanently painful jaw. One of Tate's more successful "love poems" is "Laura's Walk," in which the lady is blended with the flowers in a manner reminiscent of Robert Herrick:

I.

The Sun far sunk in his Descent,
  Laid now his Tyrant Rays aside,
When Laura to the Garden went,
  To triumph over Natures Pride.

II.

The Rose-Buds blusht with deeper Dye,
  Envying Lillies paler grew;
The Violets droopt with Fear to spie
  On Laura's Veins a richer Blew.

III.

She stoopt and gather'd as she went,
  But whilst she slaughter'd sweetly Smil'd;
As Angells tho' for Ruine sent,
  Appear with Looks serene and mild.

IV.

But now grown weary with her Toyl,
  A Garland for her Brow she frames:
Thus with proud Trophies made o'th' spoil,
  Her Conquest o'er the Spring proclaims.[13]

Of the more intellectual variety of love lyric, Tate attempted a few examples; but his development of the subject was usually slight. In "The Tear," the rich drop on Julia's face will die whether or not it falls to earth; but it can be preserved in a vial and will even be frozen—converted to a diamond—if it is put close to Julia's heart. But this last thought leads to the reflection that there is hope, for the very existence of the tear shows that the frost of Julia's heart is breaking. In "The Politicians," the title is witty; for the poem begins with the idea that, like politicians, lovers find that quarrels make the heart grow fonder; but Tate fails to develop the deeper possibilities of the metaphor. In "The Wish," Abraham Cowley had asked for his mistress, few friends, and many books; more modestly in "The Choice," Tate longs only for "a rurall Seat" and

> A private, but an active Life.
> Conscience bold, and punctual to his Charge;
> My Stock of Health, or Patience large.
> Some Books I'd have, and some Acquaintance too,
> But very good, and very few.[14]

One of the most individual poems in the 1677 volume is "Sliding on Skates in a hard Frost," in which Tate maintains a suitably mock-heroic attitude toward his rather unconventional subject:

> How well these frozen Floods now represent
> Those Chrystal Waters of the Firmament!
> Tho' Hurricanes shou'd rage, they cou'd not now
> So much as curl the solid Water's Brow;
> Proud Fleets whose stubborn Cables scarce withstood
> The Fury of the late tempestuous Flood,
> In watry Ligaments are restrain'd,
> More fast than when in binding Ooze detain'd.
> But tho their Service does at present fail,
> Our selves without the aid of Tide or Gale,
> On Keels of polisht Steel securely sail:
> From ev'ry Creek to ev'ry Point we rove,
> And in our lawless Passage swifter move
> Than Fish beneath us, or than Fowl above.[15]

Other distinctive poems in the collection include "The Hurricane," a dramatic monologue describing a shipwreck, and "The Beldam's Song," which is the spell of a witch as she stirs her pot. In these two poems Tate may well have been imitating the two "operatic" versions of Shakespeare that were highly popular during the 1670's, *The Tempest* and *Macbeth.*[16]

II *The Second Edition (1684)*

Most of the poems underwent considerable revision for the second edition, published in 1684.[17] Some of the changes seem to be mere tampering, but most are improvements, smoothing out awkward wording in the earlier version or making the meter more regular. The last five lines of the first stanza of "The Installment," for example, had been extremely rough in meter and diction. The whole stanza originally read as follows:

> Long have I Languisht in the Fire
> Of an unquenchable Desire;
> And will it not suffice thee Love,
> That I thy patient Martyr am,
> Unless thy Worship I promove,
> And proselyte others to thy Flame?
> If as a Laick-Lover ought I act,
> What canst thou more from me expect,
> Who am not gifted for a Teacher in the Sect?

In 1684 the last five lines were altered to read:

> Unless thy Worship I improve,
> Converting others to thy Flame?
> If I the Practise not neglect,
> Thou canst no more from Me expect:
> Not gifted for a Teacher in the Sect.[18]

The thirty-three poems added in 1684 are a miscellaneous collection: a few are political or occasional; some are complimentary verses to Dryden and other friends on the publication of various works; some are songs, prologues, or epilogues for the plays Tate had written between 1677 and 1684; and more than a third are translations of Roman poets. One distinctive poem is "The Battle of the B[aw]ds in the Theatre Royal, December the 3d 1680," which begins:

> Give ore ye Tilters of the Pit, give ore,
> Frighten the Boxes and your selves no more:
> Two Amazons of Scandalous renown,
> Have with dire Combat made this Field their own.

The method is that of the amused mock-heroic, not unlike the battle that concludes Pope's *Rape of the Lock;* Tate continued:

> Strong Sarcenet Scarf with Hood of Gause more slight,
> Promiscuously lay scatter'd in the fight:
> Necklace and Pendants perish't in the fray,
> And rev'rend Point that did the Art display,
> Of Ages past had now its fatal Day.[19]

Bellona finally stops the fight, "And Drury-lane all loyal Wh——es resound."

In form, the additions in 1684 are more conservative than the poems of 1677. Almost half those in the earlier volume are in couplets, about equally divided between tetrameter and pentameter. Five poems, including "Advice to a Friend" quoted above, are in couplets with alternating pentameter and tetrameter lines. Elaborate repeated stanzas appear in some of the love poems with the more extravagant conceits, such as "The Usurpers" and "The Tear." Several poems are in quatrain stanzas, and several are in stanzas made up of unequal lines after the manner of Cowley's and Flatman's odes, although in only one of these poems—the "Ode. To my Ingenious Friend, Mr. Flatman"—does Tate use the word in the title. The ode was regarded as a noble form, and Tate's restraint may be the result of the same excessive modesty that later in 1677 led him to change the names in his first play. Of the poems added in 1684, twenty-six are in pentameter couplets, three in tetrameter couplets, two in quatrains, and two in irregular stanzas.

Many of the verses in the first edition show a poet in his early twenties feeling his way and experimenting with models from the recent past. But they demonstrate a sense of poetic form and often a felicity and smoothness of expression. It is not surprising that Dryden took an interest in the young poet, collaborating with him in translations and offering him *The Second Part of Absalom and Achitophel*. The second edition of the *Poems* shows more confidence; a preference for the pentameter couplet, in which Tate was to write almost all the rest of his nondramatic verse; and an inclination toward translation.

III *Translations of Ovid and Juvenal*

In 1680 Tate joined with Dryden and Flatman, as well as Thomas Rymer, Elkanah Settle, Thomas Otway, Samuel Butler, and at least ten other poets in a translation of Ovid's *Epistles*. Although Dryden wrote the Preface ("Ovid and the Art of Translation"), translated two Epistles himself, and collaborated with the Earl of Mulgrave on a third, the project was probably that of the publisher, Jacob Tonson.[20] Tate translated "Leander to Hero," "Hero's Reply to Leander," and "Medea to Jason," of which the best is certainly the third—as Tate recognized, for he printed it but not the other two in the second edition of his *Poems*.

Ovid, a favorite in Restoration times, was admired especially for his "polite" and civilized style—"tenderly passionate and courtly," according to Dryden.[21] As the editors of the California edition point out, Dryden attempted to reproduce this style partly by omitting synaloephas (cutting off the vowel at the end of a word when the next begins with a vowel, as "th' are"); by omitting triplets; and, in "Dido to Aeneas," by composing individual couplets that are not only end-stopped but are complete units, ending with a period or its equivalent and not built in clusters of several together. Ovid's verse, Dryden would remark in 1685, has "little variety of numbers and sound"; it "is always as it were upon the Hand-gallop, and his Verse runs upon Carpet ground."[22] Dryden ended about 72 percent of the couplets in "Dido to Aeneas" with final punctuation, as opposed to about 41 percent in "Canace to Marcareus" and 47 percent in "Helen to Paris."[23] Tate used final punctuation at the end of over 80 percent of the couplets in "Hero to Leander," almost

90 percent in "Leander's Answer to Hero," and about 70 percent in "Medea to Jason." A comparison with Tate's longer couplet poems written nearest to 1680 shows that he, too, was deliberately trying to imitate Ovid's style: in "The Vision, Written in a Dangerous Fit of Sickness" (1677), only 50 percent of the couplets end with final punctuation, and final punctuation is so employed in just under 50 percent in *The Second Part of Absalom and Achitophel* (1682).

Tate and Dryden shared an enthusiasm for Ovid. In Dryden's Dedication of *Examen Poeticum* (1693), he declared that he thought his best translations were those of Ovid; his total has been estimated at more than seven thousand lines.[25] Tate, too, had high praise for Ovid and his adaptability: in 1697, he observed that "Some of our greatest Judges of Poetry have declared their Sentiments of this Author, That he is the fittest amongst the Classick Poets to be Translated into English. Indeed, he is so Natural a Writer, that he cannot fail of being agreeable in any Language he shall be made to speak."[26] About two hundred lines of Book VII of the *Metamorphoses* had appeared in Tate's 1684 *Poems*; and Tate was apparently working on a translation of more of this work as early as 1692, when Dryden wrote of "spoyl[ing] Tate's undertakings" in a letter to Tonson.[27] The first five books of the *Metamorphoses* were published under Tate's editorship in 1697 (Tate himself contributing part of Book IV) with the assurance that the remaining books were "preparing for the Press, and will be Published with all convenient Speed."[28] Although the other books were apparently never issued, Tate's remark shows that more of the translating may have been done.

In 1708 Tate collaborated with Aaron Hill in *The Celebrated Speeches of Ajax* (translated by Tate) *and Ulysses* (by Hill) from Book XIII of Ovid's *Metamorphoses.* Dryden himself had translated these speeches for his *Fables* (1700), and the sense of rivalry between the poets, suggested by Dryden's earlier letter to Tonson, appears again in the Dedication by Tate and Hill in which they express their confidence that a "Genuine Translation" will be useful. They refer to the criticism advanced against Dryden, "the Great Master of the Muses," that he mistook Ovid's manner; and, although they do not say that they subscribe to this view, they insist that at least they are not guilty of a similar error. In the following year, Tate published his translation of Ovid's *Remedy of Love*, along with an English version by others, including Dryden, of *The Art of Love*. Although Tate published fewer lines of Ovid in English than Dryden, he nevertheless had an important role in the age's translation of the Roman poet.

In 1692, Tate contributed to Dryden's translation of the *Satires* of Juvenal and Persius, which Gilbert Highet in 1954 called "still the best verse translation of Juvenal in English."[29] It is from Tate's version of Satire XV that Samuel Richardson's Clarissa quoted with praise.[30] Dryden wrote the Dedication to Dorset, the "Discourse Concerning Satire," and translated all six of Persius's and five of Juvenal's fifteen satires. He made the other assignments and, apparently, supervised the work, his collaborators being his sons, Charles and John, and Bowles, Stepney, Hervey, Congreve, Power, and Creech, each of whom did one satire, and Tate, who did Satires II and XV.[31]

Satire II begins as an attack on hypocrisy, but it soon becomes an attack upon homosexuality. From the Argument, it appears that Tate intended to gloss over some of its cruder passages: "The Poet, in this Satyr, inveighs against the Hypocrisie of the Philosophers, and Priests of his Time: the Effeminacy of Military Officers, and Magistrates. Which Corruption of Manners in General, and more Particularly of Unnatural Vices, he imputes to the Atheistical Principle that then prevail'd." Actually, however, Tate translated frankly lines that the translator in the Loeb edition, for example, thought were better left as ellipses. The high percentage of closed couplets is well suited to vigorous, forceful expression of Juvenal's wrath. The fidelity of Tate's translation of Juvenal can be judged from the relatively decorous opening lines of Satire II. The literal Loeb translation is as follows:

> I would fain flee to Sarmatia and the frozen Sea when People who ape the Curii and live like Bacchanals dare talk about morals. In the first place, they are unlearned persons, though you may find their houses crammed with plaster casts of Chrysippus; for their greatest hero is the man who has bought

a likeness of Aristotle or Pittacus, or bids his shelves preserve an original portrait of Cleanthes. Men's faces are not to be trusted; does not every street abound in gloomy-visaged debauchees? And do you rebuke foul practices, when you are yourself the most notorious delving-ground among Socratic reprobates?[32]

Tate translated the passage thus:

I'm sick of Rome, and wish myself convey'd
Where freezing Seas obstruct the Merchants Trade,
When Hypocrites read Lectures, and a Sot,
Because into a Gown and Pulpit got,
Tho surfeit-gorg'd, and reeking from the Stews,
Nothing but Abstinence for's Theam will chuse.
The Rakehells too pretend to Learning—Why?
Chrysippus Statue decks their Library.
Who makes his Closet finest is most Read:
The Dolt that with an Aristotle's Head,
Carv'd to the Life, has once adorn'd his Shelf,
Streight sets up for a Stagyrite himself.
Precise their Look, but to the Brothel come,
You'll know the Price of Philosophick Bum.[33]

The one hundred and seventy lines of Latin become two hundred and forty-five in Tate's version.

Of the three sorts of translation that Dryden distinguished in his Preface to Ovid's *Epistles*, metaphrase (word-for-word translation), paraphrase ("translation with latitude, where the author is kept in view by the translator, so as never to be lost, but his words are not so strictly followed as his sense"), and imitation (which often departs from both words and sense),[34] Tate generally paraphrased, though he occasionally imitated. An example of imitation is a couplet near the end of Satire II (11.217-18) for which there is no justification in Juvenal and which directs the Satire as a whole against atheism (as Tate had indicated in the Argument): "To what dire Cause can we assign these Crimes, / But to that reigning Atheism of the Times?" Juvenal does not mention atheism. Similarly, in Satire XV, "against the Superstition and Cruelty of the Egyptians,"

Tate indulged in a six-line parenthesis, criticizing English borrowing of false rhetoric from the French. Just a few years later such departures from the text in his translation of the Psalms provided his enemies with an opportunity to attack him.

In November, 1693, about a year after the translation of Juvenal had appeared, Tate published his own satire in *The Gentleman's Journal*.[35] Although the Juvenalian attitude was not really congenial to him, the poem succeeds fairly well as a mild imitation of it. The satire is addressed to Richard Baldwin, the publisher of Motteux and Sir Thomas Urquhart's translation of Rabelais, whom Tate familiarly calls "Dick." The poet first asserts the futility of satire, for even Rabelais, Cervantes, and Quevedo together have not reformed society. Lawyers and doctors still prey upon their clients, and clergymen profit, too:

> Has Biggottry to make a Man turn Sot,
> Or Priest-craft how to menage Fools forgot?
> Or is not, when a Pastor shifts his Place,
> A fatter Benefice the Call of Grace?
> Have you ne'er seen a Drone possess at ease
> What would provide for Ten Industrious Bees?

Tate continues with the "Plodding Citt" who becomes rich while "his graceless Son Turns Wit and Beau, drinks, whores, and is undone." Refinement of manners and speech has brought no improvement, and "Science is made Cant, and Nonsense Mystery." "Half the Gallamaufry of Mankind" consists of "Pimps, Pandars, Stallions, Buffons, Parasites, / Setters, Suborners, Sharpers, Pillory-Knights, / Cheats, Cullies, Bravoes, Cowards, Hypocrites. . . ." The poem turns finally to the vanity of human desires, and then lightly back to Rabelais: "Yet—As by witty Rabelais 'tis Exprest, / Life's Idle Droll's an entertaining Jest."

Translation and imitation seem to have been congenial occupations for Tate. His mind was not especially creative either of new ideas or of really fresh means for developing them; and he did better when the central idea and the main lines of development were suggested or laid out for him. Evidently, Dryden recognized his ability; for, when Dryden worked with a collaborator, he often chose to work with Tate.

CHAPTER 4

Early Tragedies, Dido, and King Lear

WHEN THE TWO PATENT THEATER COMPANIES were formed in 1660, their repertory was at first limited principally to pre-Civil War plays: the works of Shakespeare, Jonson, James Shirley, Philip Massinger, and especially, Beaumont and Fletcher, supplied most of the theater fare along with plays by the managers themselves, Thomas Killigrew and Davenant. Even when new plays were written and new genres developed (such as the Restoration comedy of manners and the rhymed heroic play) they were rooted in the past. Character types, especially, were often descended from Jacobean times, including, in the serious drama, the vacillating ruler, the pure and perfect heroine, the ambitious and selfish female, the Machiavellian courtier, and the noble hero great in war but naive in love. These characters were placed in plots that provided generous opportunities for conflicts of love and honor and for political scheming and military heroism. Such plays usually emphasized set speeches and toe-to-toe debate, and they exploited emotional scenes, especially those of lust or pity.

Meanwhile, new techniques and personnel were changing the theater in other ways. Davenant introduced movable scenery, consisting principally of sets of shutters that could be slid on or off the stage in grooves and could be quickly opened or closed to change scenes and to "discover" or conceal characters. As in Elizabethan times, music was worked into many plays; and, as the theater buildings became larger and the competition with and influence of foreign opera became stronger, it became increasingly important. Stage machinery was often joined with elaborate scenes, music, and singing to contribute to the spectacle, especially in such plays as *The Tempest* and *Macbeth.* Actresses replaced boys in women's roles, and old plays were adapted and new ones were written to expand the share taken by women. Among the better-known actresses who performed in Tate's plays were Elizabeth Currer as the lustful, ambitious Queen in *The Loyal General* and as Isabella in *A Duke and No Duke;* Mary Lee as Arviola, the pure but hot-tempered heroine of *The Loyal General,* and as Regan in *King Lear;* and Elizabeth Barry as a highly successful Cordelia in the much enlarged rôle given her by Tate.

I Brutus of Alba

Tate's first play, *Brutus of Alba or, The Enchanted Lovers,* had a very distinguished ancestor in *The Aeneid,* a distinguished descendant (or at least successor) in *Dido and Aeneas,* and a distinguished model in Dryden's *All for Love.* By the season of 1677-78, when *Brutus* was performed, Classical settings were in vogue. Nathaniel Lee, the chief writer of this kind of play, had begun his career in 1674 with *The Tragedy of Nero* and had followed it with one play a year with a Classical background. Dryden had deserted the exotic settings of his rhymed heroic plays for a famous Classical story in *All for Love,* and he was to collaborate with Lee in *Oedipus* in 1678 and to adapt *Troilus and Cressida* in 1679. Other playwrights—Sedley, John Crowne, Otway, and Shadwell—were also writing or adapting plays set in Classical times; and Tate, with his Classical interests, probably found such settings very much to his taste.

Sedley (in *Antony and Cleopatra*) and Dryden had used one of the most famous love-versus-duty Roman stories, and Tate chose another in the tale of Dido and Aeneas. But his confidence seems to have left him before he submitted the play, for he says in the Preface that he had intended to entitle his play "Dido and Aeneas" but that he had been dissuaded by his friends on the grounds that "it wou'd appear Arrogant to attempt any Characters that had been written by the incomparable Virgil." Hence, Aeneas became Brutus, "Prince of the Dardan Forces," and Dido became a nameless "Queen of Syracuse."

Brutus (or Brute) was the legendary great-grandson of Aeneas, who fled from Italy to Greece and thence with his son Locrinus to Britain, where he built New Troy (London). Lear was a descendant. According to Tate, Brutus has a "favourite" called "Asaracus," a name that Virgil had used for an ancestor of Aeneas and that Geoffrey of Monmouth had used both for a young nobleman of Greek and Trojan blood who was allied with Brutus in Greece and also for one of the twenty sons of Efroc, the fourth king after Brutus.[1] However, "Assaracus" also appears as a character in the pseudo-Shakespearean play *The Tragedy of Locrine,* which had been published in the Third Folio (1664), and in which he is the brother (or possibly the uncle) of Brutus.[2] Since Tate seems to have used the Third Folio for his adaptation of *Coriolanus* and perhaps for *King Lear* and *Richard II,* it seems likely that he borrowed the name from *Locrine,* a play that he would suppose to be Shakespearean.[3] Although the account of the Trojan origins of Britain had been under attack through the sixteenth and seventeenth centuries, it was still defended by some scholars, and Brutus would have seemed to many of Tate's contemporaries to have some of the reality of a historical figure.[4] Thus, *Brutus of Alba* combines the pseudo-historical accounts of the founder of Rome and of his great-grandson, the founder of Britain, probably with a suggestion from the "Shakespearean" play *Locrine.*

In Tate's version, the Queen of Syracuse falls in love with Brutus on first meeting him; but she resists her feelings and the people's wishes because she still mourns the death of her husband Argaces. Brutus, in his turn, falls in love and surrenders to his feelings despite the urgings of his friend Asaracus, his responsibility to his destiny and his son Locrinus, and his duty to his dead wife. When Brutus pleads his case with Dido, his appeal falls on deaf ears until, in Act III, the storm disperses the hunting party and chases the lovers to a cave where they sleep together. Afterward, the lovers vacillate, trying to choose among the alternatives of suicide, of continuing together despite Brutus's destiny, and of separating. Even the spectacle of

Asaracus's committing suicide in Brutus's presence is not enough to persuade the hero to leave, and it requires the appearance of Asaracus's ghost and the Queen's resigning herself to the inevitable to part them. When Brutus has left, the Queen dies of a broken heart, and her maid, Amarante, stabs herself.

Because this story provided little activity, Tate filled out the play with four minor actions. One of these is a secondary love affair between Asaracus and Amarante. Another is the story of Soziman, the general of the city, who is rather perfunctorily linked to the second group of lovers by being enamored of Amarante, and is more substantially connected with principal lovers both by hating Brutus because Locrinus has killed his son and by plotting to overthrow the Queen. Soziman is employed in the plot to overthrow the Queen by the ambassadors of the Agrigentine king, who, though he never appears on stage, attempts to acquire the Queen's throne by marrying her and, when he is unsuccessful, by threatening war and by scheming through Soziman. In his turn, Soziman employs the witch Ragusa and her four assistants, who raise the storm that drives Brutus and the Queen together and who then lace their drink with an aphrodisiac. (Thereby Tate removes from the lovers some of the blame for their actions—a point that is emphasized in the subtitle *The Enchanted Lovers.*) Ragusa also prophesies dire events and curses the Queen's house; she gives Soziman a poisoned bracelet which destroys him at the moment of his triumph; and she herself is destroyed at the end of the play because her time has expired.

Tate was evidently influenced by Dryden's *All for Love* in the way he developed his material. Not only are both blank-verse plays based on Classical love stories, but the pressures that Antony undergoes from Ventidius and Cleopatra are similar to those Brutus must undergo from Asaracus and the Queen. Soziman, though he is cruder and more villainous than Alexas, is also a subtle schemer; like Caesar in *All for Love,* the Agrigentine king threatens through his ambassadors but does not appear himself; Locrinus is used as a means of appealing to the hero's sense of duty as the children of Antony and Octavia are used in Dryden's play; and the number of important characters is strictly limited: there are about seven in each play.

Although Ragusa and her companions are unlike the witches in *Macbeth* in that they are curious or odd rather than dangerous, they, like Shakespeare's witches, influence the course of action; they recite their charms; they forecast the future; and their dialogue occasionally suggests Shakespeare's play or Davenant's adaptation of it. On one occasion, for example, they consider what they will do to a ship when they overtake it, much as the witches in *Macbeth* gloat over the suffering they anticipated for the "master o'the *Tiger*."[5] Ragusa and her Women preparing their charms at the end of the third act are reminiscent of *Macbeth*:

> *Rag.* Around me, and I'll deal to each her dole.
> There's an Elf-Lock, Tooth of Hermaphrodite
> A brace of Mandrakes digg'd in Fairy Ground,
> A Lampray's Chain, Snakes Eggs, dead sparks of Thunder
> Quencht in its passage through the cold mid Air,
> A Mermaids Fin, A Cockatrice's Comb,
> Wrapt i'th' dri'd Cawl of a Brat still-born: burn'em—
> In whispers take the rest, which nam'd aloud
> Would fright the Day, and force another Storm.[6]

Charles Lamb included over one hundred lines from the witch passages in his *Extracts from Garrick Plays* supplementary to his *Specimens of English Dramatic Poets*.[7]

The witches also contribute to the spectacular element in *Brutus of Alba*. Among the more detailed stage directions are: Ragusa "Falls flat on her Face, as she lies two deformed Spirits descend, and whisper in each Ear"; "A Dance of Masquers, during which a dark Storm gathers. Lightning and Thunder. . . . Ragusa appears in the Storm. . . . An Owl Cries"; later "A Tune of horrour play'd, after which a Dwarf Spirit rises"; having told Ragusa her end has come, it "Descends," like the spirits invoked in *Macbeth*, and Ragusa "vanishes."[8] Other scenes are also spectacular. In Act II, for example, Dido is revealed at the tomb of her late husband: "The Scene opening [i.e., the shutters that formed the back of the previous scene—at court—being drawn apart] discovers Argaces Tomb deckt with Armory and Wreaths of Lawrel; a Priestess clad in White, at each Corner, they round the Tomb scattering Flowers and singing the following Stanza's. The Queen kneels at some distance." After the song is sung and Brutus has pleaded his case, "Ghost of Agaces [*sic*] rises on the one side of the Tomb, Ghost of Eudemia [Brutus's wife] on the other." The next scene is headed "A Desart. At some distance a Fountain with the Statue of Diana."[9] And the play ends spectacularly: in the last thirty lines the Queen dies, Amarante stabs herself and dies, the ambassadors arrive, and "Enter Soziman [who has been poisoned by Raguas's bracelet] with his Cloaths disorder'd, Stabbing himself with a Dagger in each Hand." The Epilogue is then spoken by "Ragusa rising from under the Stage."[10]

There are faults in *Brutus of Alba* that are typical of a first play. The exposition is clumsy: Soziman's declaration in Act II, for example, that he loves Amarante and that he will seek the help of Ragusa, who has not been mentioned previously, is unexpected. And there is an incoherence in the last act, as if the playwright was not fully able to handle his material. Locrinus is unnecessary to the plot, and Tate is not entirely successful in making Soziman and Ragusa seem essential to the love story. The style, too, is often stiff and forced, especially in the quick give-and-take of conversation. On occasion, however, Tate's lines show insight and conciseness, as in the Queen's "My swelling Passions crowd each other's way, / And pressing all for utterance, all are mute."[11] Or in her Websterian "From Shades to Court, from Court to Shades I fly, / But bear my Torment with me where I goe, / Thought-rackt and Restless as a Murd'rer's Soul!"[12]

In his Preface, Tate complained about critics who condemn a play merely because it is learned or because a dance is poorly performed. Apparently, *Brutus of Alba* failed in the theater; but it had at least one descendant besides *Dido and Aeneas:* in 1696, an opera called *Brutus of Alba; or, Augusta's Triumph,* attributed to George Powell with music by Daniel Purcell, was performed at Dorset Garden. This was a sequel to Tate's play, using similar names (Brutus, Amarante, Arsaracus [*sic*] Locrinus, Ragusa, and Soziman); and it is said to have borrowed scenery from Dryden's *Albion and Albanius.*[13]

II Dido and Aeneas

Although *Dido and Aeneas* was Henry Purcell's first substantial score for the theater, it is generally considered his masterpiece. Moreover, Eric W. White in *The Rise of English Opera* assigned it an important role in the history of music when he called it "the first true English opera" because in it composer replaced playwright as the dominant figure in the collaboration, and the latter became librettist.[14] Much has been written about *Dido and Aeneas* in recent years because of renewed interest in Purcell, whose tercentenary was celebrated in 1959; and Tate has received considerable praise from musicians and music historians for his share, subordinate though it may have been.

In *Henry Purcell 1659-1695 Essays on His Music,* the British tenor Peter Pears remarked that "Nahum Tate knew what he was about, and he gave Purcell verses of a neutral, passive quality which were fair game for a real composer"; E. W. White referred to "the operatic masterpiece that Tate and Purcell planned and created together"; and Imogen Holst observed that "the astonishing unity of *Dido and Aeneas* is often mentioned, but Tate's share in it has seldom been acknowledged. He was Purcell's only real librettist in our sense of the word." She even had praise for the notorious example of Tate's good libretto but dubious poetry: "Thus on the fatal banks of Nile, / Weeps the deceitful Crocodile."[15] In another recent book, *Henry Purcell & the Restoration Theatre,* Robert E. Moore has discussed the opera at length and has given Tate credit for keeping the story "simple"; for a "variety and skilful grouping of . . . moods and feelings"; and for writing verse that states the mood rather than creates it and that remains subordinate to the music.[16]

The opera has little apparent relation to *Brutus of Alba.* All the names are different, and Tate does not seem to have used the dialogue of his tragedy. The only borrowing of importance is the witches, who are substituted for Virgil's Classical deities as they had been in the play. The story itself is very simple. In Act I, Belinda (the Amarante of *Brutus* and the Anna of Virgil), the Chorus, and then Aeneas himself attempt to persuade Dido to return the hero's love; but they are unsuccessful. Act II is in two scenes: in the first, the Sorceress and her two witches plot to separate the lovers (rather than drive them together) by a storm and to send an "Elf" in the form of Mercury to order Aeneas to continue his journey; and, in the second scene, this plan is carried out. Act III is at "the Ships," a location not used in *Brutus of Alba*. The Sailors and the Chorus set the mood; the witches arrive to celebrate their success ("Elissas [*sic*] bleeds to Night, and Carthage Flames tomorrow"); though Aeneas weakens, Dido insists that he leave; and then, slowly, Dido dies.

Tate is adept at changing the mood of the verse. The first act, for example, ends with the following lyric by the Chorus:

> To the Hills and the Vales, to the Rocks and the Mountains
> To the Musical Groves, and the cool Shady Fountains.
> Let the Triumphs of Love and of Beauty be Shown,
> Go Revel ye Cupids, the day is your own.[17]

To this light and joyful mood we may contrast the somber, trochaic verse of the witches at the beginning of the second act:

> Weyward Sisters, you that Fright
> The Lonely Traveller by Night.
> Who like dismal Ravens Crying,
> Beat the Windowes of the Dying.
> Appear at my call, and share in the Fame,
> Of a Mischief shall make all Carthage to flame.

In this version of the Dido-Aeneas story the lovers do not sleep together but are merely separated by the storm, and it is not made clear how Dido dies. Since the opera was written for performance by the girls at the School for Young Gentlewomen at Chelsea run by the dancing master Josias Priest, one supposes that the first omission was made in the interest of decorum and that Dido dies of a broken heart and not, as Kirsten Flagstad played the role at the Mermaid Theatre in

1951-53, by stabbing herself.[18] Professional singers probably performed the two male roles,[19] but otherwise the opera is controlled by the conditions of its original production: the cast is largely feminine, and there are seventeen dances. Performance takes about an hour; little use is made of spectacular effects; and the orchestra consists of only two violins, viola, bass, and continuo. Although Purcell's score was not printed until 1841, Thomas Durfey's Epilogue was published in 1690, thereby establishing the latest possible date for the opera; the libretto appeared in an undated pamphlet of which only a single copy seems to have survived.[20]

The first professional performance did not come until 1700, when the addition of masques to comedies was in vogue. Then the work was fragmented and played as "The Loves of Dido and Aeneas, a Mask, in Four Musical Entertainments" incorporated into Charles Gildon's adaptation of *Measure for Measure.*[21] The staging is more elaborate, and the dances are cut. The first of the four "Entertainments" (Act I of the opera) is performed before Angelo at the end of the first act and seems to him "to Sing only Isabella's Beauty" to his "Enchanted Ears": it is, then, actually worked into the story of the play. The Second Entertainment is again before Angelo, after he has been rejected by Isabella; it consists principally of the two scenes of the opera's Act II, but in the wrong order (in the printed text at least), thereby making the Sorceress plan what has already been carried out. There is also a passage in which the two friends argue the hero's decision for him, one supporting the claims of Love and the other of Honor. This passage is not in other editions of the libretto or musical text; it provides a firm ending for the scene, which, it has been pointed out, is otherwise incomplete musically. White suggests that the passage might have been suppressed in the original performance because it would have called for additional male roles.[22] Angelo sees in this Entertainment, not the parallel between Aeneas's duty and his, but rather a parallel between the storm which drives the lovers together (he thinks of Virgil, not of the opera) and Claudio's "danger" as a storm which will enable Angelo to seduce Isabella.

The Third Entertainment (the opera's Act III) is before Angelo at the end of Act III. The fourth, which concludes the play, is the two-scene Prologue (with shepherds, shepherdesses, and Classical deities) that was apparently part of the original opera (for it appears in Tate's libretto), although there is some doubt whether the music for it is Henry Purcell's. The opera (or masque) was performed as an afterpiece twice in 1704,[23] but it seems to have been forgotten thereafter until the nineteenth century, when its rise to its present eminence began.

III The Loyal General

No source for the complex plot of *The Loyal General* has been found. The setting is simply "Greece," where a weak King is opposed by his traitorous and adulterous Queen, who schemes to obtain the succession for her daughter Edraste. Edraste, however, lacks ambition and is much attached to her half-sister, the beautiful Arviola. The male villain—strongly reminiscent of Sosius in *Brutus of Alba*, except that he is even cleverer—is named Escalus; he has been the Queen's lover, but, because he has been replaced in her affections by the young and naive Pisander, he now plots against her as well as against the King. Escalus's confidante is his sister Myrrhoe, who is almost as clever as he. The hero is the young general Theocrin, who is loved both by Edraste and Arviola, and who himself loves the latter. His rival for Arviola's hand is the neighboring prince Abardanes, who is helped by his clever adviser Sossicles.

Although many of the characters are conventional, some of them seem also to prefigure the Shakespearean characters that Tate was to work with in the months after he had finished *The Loyal General*. The King, for example, though he is weak and vacillating like Dryden's Boabdelin, has something of Richard II's moodiness:

> So various are the Transports of his Rage,
> That with each minute his Resolves are chang'd:
> Sometimes defies aloud the Rebel Pow'rs,
> Threatning swift Vengeance; then despairs agen,
> And cries all's lost, the Fates are Factious too!
> Thus tost with Doubts, and starting from his Chair

> He grasps his Scepter, cries I have thee still;
> Nor shall the Furies wrest thee: then o'th' sudden
> Disdaining casts it from him; thou'rt a Serpent,
> Away infectious Rod, thou fir'st my Hand.[24]

Like Lear, he is old and would like to give up the throne; and, like Lear in Tate's adaptation, he adopts a solitary, retired life at the end of the play. His beautiful, devoted daughter Arviola, doubtful of her lover's faithfulness and in danger of being abducted by the villanous Escalus, is in somewhat the same position as Tate's Cordelia, who insists that Edgar demonstrate his faithfulness to her and is very nearly abducted by Edmund's henchmen. *The Loyal General* seems to have been the link—the experience, as far as Tate is concerned—whereby some of the conventional situations and characters of Restoration drama made their way into the adaptation of *King Lear*.

The melodramatic plot is full of turns of fortune and shifts of allegiance: Tate's attention is on rapid and sensational action, situations of extreme emotion, and stage spectacle. Act V, for example, opens with Theocrin, who is betrothed to Arviola but is now rejected by both her and the King, despairing and drinking poison. Hardly has he done so when officers arrive with news that the army will support his cause; but they arrive too late, and they can only take him to a nearby hermit's cell to wait for his death. At the hut, Edraste, disguised in the clothing of a youth, is helping the hermit consecrate a tomb; she recognizes Theocrin when he arrives but is not recognized by him. Next, Escalus attempts to abduct Arviola for Abardanes, but she is rescued by Theocrin's officers, and Myrrhoe is wounded. As the would-be abductors flee past the hut, Theocrin kills them, but Edraste is wounded. In the concluding scene, Edraste dies in Theocrin's arms, whereupon Arviola enters and, misunderstanding the situation, stabs herself. She and Theocrin (who is finally near death from the poison he took) live long enough to see Myrrhoe enter "bloody" and die. After their death, the King arrives with Escalus, who has persuaded the King of his faithfulness and is about to be rewarded when news is brought that the Queen has committed suicide and has exposed Escalus, who is led off to execution. The King dons a hermit's robes as the play ends.

The stage directions show a fondness for "discovery" scenes. Act II begins with the Queen's new favorite Pisander alone on the stage. After "Soft Musick, [the] Bower Opening discovers the Queen Splendid and youthfully Attir'd"; Pisander tactfully mistakes her for a goddess. Later, when Myrrhoe brings Abardanes to see Arviola, the scene is drawn to reveal the lovers Arviola and Theocrin together. And the device is used a third time when Escalus reveals the love affair of the Queen and Pisander to the King: "Scene drawing, discovers the Grotto. Queen and Pisander amorously seated in a Bowr."[25] They listen to a song before they are interrupted. When Tate began Act IV of *King Lear* with a new scene headed "A Grotto. Edmund and Regan amorously Seated, list'ning to Musick," he probably had in mind not only much the same effect but even the same scenery that had been used for *The Loyal General*.

The style of most of the play is bombastic. However, the complex, fast-moving plot compelled Tate to keep his eye on the purpose of each passage; as a result, the speeches are more direct than those in *Brutus of Alba*. At the beginning of Act V, as Theocrin soliloquizes about taking poison, Tate relinquishes his bombast for melancholy reflection in unaffected language:

> The Storm is husht, the Winds breath out their last,
> The Thunders too in feebler Volleys die;
> All Night they humour'd my Complaints; but now
> The Day intrudes, the dear Confusion's vanisht,
> And all the ruffled Elements return
> To their dull Order. Shroud thy hated Light,
> Thou rising Sun, nor summon with such speed,
> Th'o'rlabour'd World to th' Toils of a new day!
> Why flatter'd Mortals, will ye wake to Cares,
> When Sleep in kind Delusion may divert
> Your pensive Minds with pleasing Images.
> A Dream sets free the Captive, can restore
> Lost Fields to Souldiers, and wreckt Merchants Wealth;

In Dreams the Exile Visits his dear home,
And o'r the sparkling Bowl relates at large
His past Distresses to his won'dring Friends!
The lover too [,] the sad forsaken Lover,
May dream and feign the falsest Mistress true.
O for a gentle Slumber, that wou'd thus
Delude my Griefs, . . .[26]

Scott-Thomas points out that the lines on sleep are reminiscent of Henry IV's well-known soliloquy, but Tate did not borrow from it verbally.[27]

In his Preface to *The Loyal General*, addressed to his friend Edward Tayler, Tate shows that he has been reading Shakespeare. After defending poetry against the charge of its "Insignificancy to the World" on the grounds that it requires many rare qualities to make a poet and that it is very difficult to write poetry well, Tate undertakes to discuss Shakespeare, ostensibly because Tayler has wished "to see the Common Places of our Shakespear, compar'd with the most famous of the Ancients." Tate quotes Dryden's remark about Shakespeare's "largest and most comprehensive Soul" and asserts that he thinks Shakespeare's learning was greater than is generally conceded: "I am sure he never touches on a Roman Story, but the Persons, the Passages, the Manners, the Circumstances, the Ceremonies, all are Roman. And what Relishes yet of a more exact Knowledge, you do not only see a Roman in his Heroe, but the particular Genius of the Man, without the least mistake of his Character, given him by their best Historians." As examples, he cites the Antony of *Antony and Cleopatra* and Brutus from *Julius Caesar*.

Most important, however, " 'tis evident that no man was better studied [than Shakespeare] in Men and Things. . . . He was a most diligent Spie upon Nature, trac'd her through her darkest Recesses, pictur'd her in her just Proportion and Colours; in which Variety 'tis impossible that all shou'd be equally pleasant, 'tis sufficient that all be proper." Examples are cited from *Troilus and Cressida; Henry the Sixth, Part III;* and *Richard III.* Although Shakespeare "is often insipid where he is careless, [and] many Things he wrote in a hurry," he equals the Ancients in "his more elaborate Scenes." Most of

Tate's remarks were anticipated by Dryden's observations, but the examples are his own. It is evident that he has been reading and thinking about Shakespeare with the encouragement of such friends as Tayler, Thomas Boteler (to whom he dedicated *King Lear*), and, presumably, Dryden, who wrote the Prologue for *The Loyal General*.

IV King Lear

It might seem to the modern reader that, if Tate had really admired Shakespeare, he should not have adapted his plays. But the writers of the Neoclassic age thought otherwise: if they admired an author—as they admired the ancients—they imitated him, trying to write as they thought he would have written had he been their contemporary. If the author was an English playwright, this practice often meant fitting his work to the stage conditions of the day and adjusting his plot, characters, and language to contemporary taste. Along with Dryden and Davenant, who fancied himself Shakespeare's poetical son, Tate made up the trio of those Restoration admirers of Shakespeare who practiced most extensively the sincere form of flattery of keeping the works of the dead polished and up to date. Although we may feel that the adapters were arrogant in assuming that they could "improve" Shakespeare, we should recognize that they were also humble enough to see the superiority of his works to their own unaided efforts—an attitude that is conveyed in the Prefaces both to Tate's *Loyal General* and to his adaptations.

Between 1660 and 1700, at least twenty-three of Shakespeare's plays were performed in London. About half of these were staged during the first few years after the return of Charles II, when there was a shortage of new plays. Most of them were adapted in the typical Restoration manner: some scenes were omitted and new ones were added; male roles were reduced, but female roles were often increased; and the lines were both cut and reworded in accordance with Restoration taste. Then for a decade there was little altering of Shakespeare, until, during the fifty-two months from December, 1677, to March, 1682, eight plays based upon Shakespeare were performed for the first time since before the Civil War; and *Romeo and Juliet* and *King Lear,* which had appeared previously but without much success, were revived in new and successful adaptations.

All ten of the adaptations made around 1680 were historical or pseudohistorical in their setting (*Romeo and Juliet* was placed in ancient Rome), and all but *Cymbeline* were tragedies. Three reasons may be advanced for the renewed interest in Shakespearean drama of this kind. First, serious playwrights were moving from the rhymed heroic play to a more realistic kind of drama written in blank verse and often dealing with Classical subjects; taste in the current theater, in other words, was moving toward Shakespeare in this respect. Second, several of the leading dramatists, including Dryden and Shadwell, set an example by using Shakespearean materials. And third, the theater was becoming increasingly political after 1677: more and more the serious drama reflected on contemporary political affairs; and Shakespeare's history plays and tragedies, with a realism that was strikingly in contrast with the fantasy of the heroic plays, were easily made to comment on such matters. It seems to have been Shakespeare's strong sense of order, loyalty, obedience, and the dangers of Civil War and his firmly drawn, often historical background that drew the adapters especially to his dramas at this time.

However, political considerations had a minimum of direct effect on Tate's first adaptation, *The History of King Lear*. The adapter made four major alterations in the play. He added a whole new plot strand—the love of Edgar and Cordelia—which resulted in about one hundred and sixty lines of new dialogue in the first and third acts.[28] He provided a happy ending in which Lear and Cordelia are rescued at the last moment by Edgar and Albany; Lear and Gloucester (who also survives) announce their retirement; and Edgar and Cordelia are betrothed and will begin their happy reign. The Fool is omitted from the play. And Edmund is elevated to the role of principal villain in the tragedy: his soliloquy "Thou Nature art my Goddess" is the first speech in the play; more is made of his adulterous affairs with Lear's daughters; and he plots an abduction-with-rape of Cordelia. In addition, the language is considerably altered, and the adaptation is cut, so that, even with Tate's additions, it is only about three-fourths as long as the original. Shakespeare's three scenes on the heath containing four hundred and six lines are reduced to two scenes and two hundred and ten lines, and the excisions would probably have been even more substantial in these scenes if Tate had not admired the language of Poor Tom.

The stage success of Tate's version is unquestioned; it survived even rival versions made by David Garrick and George Coleman in the eighteenth century. Like his friend Dr. Johnson, Arthur Murphy approved of the happy ending: "the Circumstances of Lear's Restoration, and the virtuous Edgar's Alliance with the amiable Cordelia, must always call forth those gushing Tears which are swelled and ennobled by a virtuous Joy."[29] In 1770, Francis Gentleman took a similar view; after mentioning such flaws as the "rather disjointed" plot and the imperfect unity of time and place, he observed that "the catastrophe, so happily conceived by Tate, atones for all the unreformed irregularities; and, we may venture to say, that from his hands the public have received a dramatic piece, which appeals so powerfully to the passions, that when performed with suitable abilities, it proves rather a degree of painful pleasure, and shrinks nature back upon herself."[30] However, not all eighteenth-century critics approved: Addison felt that the play had "lost half its Beauty" by being given a happy ending; and Coleman criticized Tate's adaptation harshly in the Preface to his own (1768), which omitted the love story but retained the happy ending.[31]

The Romantic critics were antagonistic. Charles Lamb denounced the happy ending as an unsuitable end to Lear's sufferings. Although Leigh Hunt felt that the Fool was "out of date," he expressed the indignation of his generation and later when he objected that

> . . . a mere rhymer [Tate], whose dullness has become proverbial, should create whole scenes of his own and adorn them with a few extracts from Shakespeare, that he should turn the current of our poet's feeling into scanty sprinklings over his own barren fancy and then cry out, "How fertile I am!"—is really a violation of a man's literary property. . . .

> The original *King Lear* is a deep tragedy: it is entirely occupied with the distress arising from violent passions, and with awful lessons on parental partiality; but Tate (amorous soul) must divide this interest, and accordingly he has introduced a love-scene in which the admirable Cordelia, the pattern of filial piety, is made to forget her old, houseless, distracted father, whom she is wildly seeking, and not only to find time for listening to a lover, but to retire with him into a cave in order to dry her clothes before she goes any further. Cordelia, in this instance therefore, becomes a lover who sacrifices her filial to her amatory tenderness, and is a different character from the original Cordelia, whose whole imagination is filled with one great, pathetic, and disinterested idea. Shakespeare made his play end unhappily, because he knew that real nature required such a catastrophe; but Tate (impassioned soul) must have a marriage between the lovers at the end, and the old father must give them his blessing. . . . It appears to me . . . that the old age of Lear has been too much shattered by his repeated madness to survive a second change of fortune, and that the exhaustion of which he dies in Shakespeare is in every respect natural and unavoidable.[32]

Hunt wrote in 1808 (and Lamb in 1811); the tragic ending was restored in 1823; the Fool, played by an actress, reappeared in 1838; and the love story was omitted in the same year. Tate's version has received very little praise since then, although some critics, including A. C. Bradley, have expressed their unhappiness over the death of Cordelia.[33]

Hunt preferred the "real nature" of Shakespeare's ending as opposed to Tate's, evidently assuming that there must be a choice between the plays. He was justified in this assumption because in his day it was a real issue as to which version belonged on the stage. But the contest has long since been decided in Shakespeare's favor, and today we can afford to consider separately the two dramatizations of the story. Tate's *King Lear*, though it is a part of the stage history of Shakespeare's play and had a significant role in keeping Shakespeare in the theater, was not written to compete with its predecessor; and, except perhaps in the minds of a few critics, it did not *compete* with the original for the seventeenth- and eighteenth-century theater audiences. The adaptation, then, was judged not in terms of what Shakespeare accomplished but in terms of what the adapter himself had done with the characters and story. Shakespeare's is, of course, much the greater work; but Tate's is nevertheless a very good play with different ends and, quite properly, different means.

In *The History of King Lear,* Tate tells an absorbing story that is more or less conventional in character relationships, though, since it is neither tragedy nor comedy and only vaguely "history," it is unconventional in genre. The tale recounts the suffering of two lovers and their families—their fathers and their siblings. Like the conventional fathers of Romantic story and drama, the old gentlemen of Tate's play misjudge their children; they favor their vicious offspring and reject those who are loving and deserving. After considerable suffering, the fathers realize their error; the good brother slays the evil brother; the evil sisters poison each other; the virtuous sister is rescued by the good brother; and the two fathers, together with a virtuous uncle (Kent), retire, leaving the future to the next generation. We are reminded of the typical Restoration or eighteenth-century comedy, in which the older generation settles a fortune on its heirs. In Tate's Preface, the adapter refers to his rather unconventional play as a tragedy with a happy outcome, and he quotes from Dryden's Dedication to *The Spanish Friar* to justify such endings. In fact it seems that Tate's eye was upon success in the theater rather than upon the critics and their rules, for the play violates the unities of time and place; and, in having a love story added to the double plot of the original—even a unifying love story—the author pays very dubious respects to the unity of action.

Tate's alterations hang together well. The love affair helps to unite the stories of Lear and Gloucester and to motivate Cordelia's cold answer to Lear; for, as she makes clear, she is deliberately unresponsive in order to avoid marrying Burgundy. Since this love affair becomes the heart of the play, there is less place for Lear's suffering upon the heath and no place for Shakespeare's bitter Fool. The emphasis upon Edmund's treachery in the first speech of the play and upon Cordelia's clear motivation for deceiving Lear prepare us for the fathers' rejection of their children; Cordelia's not marrying the King of France results in her having no place to go; and Edgar's love for her motivates his remaining nearby. Quite uncharacteristically, Tate boasts of his ingenuity in these matters in his Dedication, and he adds that the love plot also heightens "the distress of the story." His pride is justified.

Despite Tate's boast, his Dedication contains high praise of Shakespeare.[34] He begins with his own "Zeal for all the Remains of Shakespear." He praises the mad scenes in *King Lear:* "The Images and Language are so odd and surprizing, and yet so agreeable and proper, that whilst we grant that none but Shakespear cou'd have form'd such Conceptions, yet we are satisfied that they were the only Things in the World that ought to be said on those Occasions." Tate concludes by saying that, in the new parts of the play, he has tried to imitate Shakespeare's style. To a modern reader, it does not seem that he has done so successfully, but in Tate's age writers regarded the Elizabethan style as inferior to their own in sophistication and regularity. As Tate says in his Dedication, "I found the whole . . . a Heap of Jewels, unstrung and unpolisht; yet so dazling in their Disorder, that I soon perceiv'd I had seiz'd a Treasure." Imitating Shakespeare's language meant, therefore, writing in a relatively unpolished style.

The soliloquy with which Tate's play opens is a good example of what the adapter thought he should do with Shakespeare's language; for, as we might expect of the first major speech in the play, it has been carefully wrought.[35] In Tate's version, Edmund says:

> Thou Nature art my Goddess, to thy Law
> My Services are bound, why am I then
> Depriv'd of a Son's Right because I came not
> In the dull Road that custom has prescrib'd?
> Why Bastard, wherefore Base, when I can boast 5
> A Mind as gen'rous and a Shape as true
> As honest Madam's Issue? why are we
> Held Base, who in the lusty stealth of Nature
> Take fiercer Qualities than what compound
> The scanted Births of the stale Marriage-bed? 10
> Well then, legitimate Edgar, to thy right

Of Law I will oppose a Bastard's Cunning.
Our Father's Love is to the Bastard Edmund
As to Legitimate Edgar: with success
I've practis'd yet on both their easie Natures: 15
Here comes the old Man chaf't with th' Information
Which last I forg'd against my Brother Edgar,
A Tale so plausible, so boldly utter'd
And heightned by such lucky Accidents,
That now the slightest circumstance confirms him, 20
And Base-born Edmund spight of Law inherits.[36]

In the Third Folio of Shakespeare, the soliloquy is as follows:

Thou Nature art my Goddess, to thy Law
My services are bound, wherefore should I
Stand in the plague of custome, and permit
The curiosity of Nations, to deprive me?
For that I am some twelve, or fourteen Moonshines 5
Lag of a brother? Why bastard? Wherefore base?
When my Dimensions are as well compact,
My mind as generous, and my shape as true
As honest Madam's issue? Why brand they us
With base? With baseness Bastardy? Base, Base? 10
Who in the lusty stealth of Nature, take
More composition, and fierce quality,
Then doth within a dull stale tyred bed
Go [to] the creating a whole tribe of Fops
Got 'tween a sleep, and wake? Well then, 15
Legitimate Edgar, I must have your land,
Our Father's love, is to the Bastard Edmund,
As to th'legitimate: fine word: Legitimate.
Well, my Legitimate, if this letter speed,
And my invention thrive, Edmund the base 20
Shall to[p] th'Legit[i]mate: I grow, I prosper:
Now gods, stand up for Bastards.

Tate avoids such peculiar phrases as "plague of custome," "curiosity of Nations," and "twelve, or fourteen Moonshines Lag"; and he also avoids Edmund's playing with the words themselves, "Base," "Bastard," and "legitimate." He rewrites Shakespeare's lines 2b-6, cutting them by almost half to a little over two lines (2b-4); he omits Shakespeare's line 7, probably as redundant with the second part of line 8; and he excludes lines 14-15, also, probably for their seeming repetition. Shakespeare's lines 19-21, on the other hand, which explain what Edmund is going to do, are expanded (Tate's 15-21); and they state his plan much more explicitly, along with the observation on the part of the probability-conscious adapter that "lucky Accidents" have helped Edmund's not overly credible plot. Shakespeare's last line is excluded, perhaps because it seemed indecorous, but more likely because the line might be taken to refer to Charles's illegitimate son the Duke of Monmouth, who was one of the chief Whig candidates for the succession. To begin a play with a villainous bastard was one thing; but to allow him to cry "Now gods, stand up for Bastards!" would seem most impolitic under the circumstances.

Presumably, it is with Shakespeare's lines as Tate had altered them that he wanted his own lines to harmonize, and such love talk as Edgar's is nearer the deliberate statement of Tate's style, though it may seem entirely out of harmony with the figurative expression of Shakespeare:

> Has Heaven then weigh'd the merit of my Love,
> Or is't the raving of my sickly Thought?
> Cou'd Burgundy forgoe so rich a Prize
> And leave her to despairing Edgar's Arms?
> Have I thy Hand Cordelia, do I clasp it,
> The Hand that was this minute to have join'd
> My hated Rivals? do I kneel before thee
> And offer at thy feet my panting Heart?
> Smile, Princess, and convince me, for as yet
> I doubt, and dare not trust the dazling Joy. (I. i. 188–97)

Although Tate's *King Lear* has much good theater and has been said to possess "more visual interest than any of the other non-operatic adaptations,"[37] it is the least merely theatrical of Tate's plays. The scenes of pity and the two dramatic onstage rescues by Edgar emerge naturally from the love story which, as we have seen, has many other important functions in the structure of the play and in the motivation of the characters. Similarly, Tate must have been tempted to take advantage of the political potentialities of a story in which an elderly king suffers dreadful consequences after disturbing the natural course of succession and in which a rebellious, illegitimate son must be put down. Tate, who resisted the temptation, deserves Ward's praise as "a painstaking and talented writer who, with enduring success, adapted *King Lear*."[38]

CHAPTER 5

Political Tragedy and Satire

ALTHOUGH POLITICAL AFFAIRS had little effect upon *The History of King Lear,* they influenced Tate's handling of *Richard II;* they probably led him to choose *Coriolanus* for adaptation; and, of course, they provided the occasion for *The Second Part of Absalom and Achitophel.* In September, 1678, Titus Oates brought forward his notorious allegations concerning a Catholic plot against the crown. According to Oates, it was planned by Catholics at home and abroad that Charles would be murdered along with many of his Protestant subjects; that his Catholic brother, James, Duke of York, would be placed upon the throne; that a French army be used to help accomplish these measures; and that the kingdom would be forcibly converted to Roman Catholicism.

Amid the political and religious uncertainties of the time and the fear of French power, the story seemed credible to many; and when Sir Edmund Berry Godfrey, the magistrate who took Oates's depositions as to the truth of his allegations, was found murdered, still more people were convinced. Many persons went about armed to protect themselves against Papists, and the inventor of the "Godfrey dagger" is said to have sold three thousand copies of his creation in one day.[1] Parliament met a few days after the murder of Godfrey. When King Charles showed himself skeptical of the plot and unwilling to move against the Catholics, Parliament itself undertook to act. Except for the Duke of York, Catholics were forbidden to sit in either house; and, in November, the question was raised as to whether the duke should be excluded from the succession in order to ensure that the next ruler would be a Protestant and to remove from Catholics the temptation to commit regicide.

Charles opposed this policy of exclusion, and for the next two and one-half years Parliament, under the leadership of the Earl of Shaftesbury, was opposed to the king on this issue. The political situation worsened rapidly: the queen was accused of plotting to murder her husband; the Commons impeached Charles's chief minister, the Earl of Danby, who went to the Tower of London; a bill was proposed excluding the Duke of York from the succession, and Parliament had to be dismissed before the proposal could come to a third reading; James himself was forced into exile, first to Brussels and then to Scotland; the king's illegitimate son, the Duke of Monmouth, was put forward as a rival candidate with claims that he was really legitimate; new plots were "discovered"; and in November of 1680 the Commons approved (and the Lords defeated after a long debate) the second exclusion bill. It was against this background—in December and January—that Tate's *Richard II* was performed and banned.

Most of the playwrights, including Dryden, Otway, Edward Ravenscroft, Crowne, and Tate, sided with the king's supporters, the Tories. It was in their interest to do so, for the court supported the theater; but their convictions were not necessarily opposed to their interest. From the Tory point of view, the Whigs were threatening another civil war such as that of less than forty years earlier. By interfering with the succession, they would undermine royal authority and would in effect depose a king.

The dangers of this course of action became a theme of Tory drama, especially of Shakespeare adapted. Dryden pointed out the dangers of disobedience in *Troilus and Cressida*; Otway warned of the consequents of civil war in *Caius Marius*, which is *Romeo and Juliet* in a background of Roman factional strife; Ravenscroft said that his *Titus Andronicus* showed "how Rogues may frame a Plot that shall deceive and destroy both the Honest and the Wise";[2] and Crowne made two plays out of selections from the three parts of Shakespeare's *Henry VI*, with emphasis on Jack Cade's rebellion, the sufferings of civil war, and the evils of Roman Catholicism. The dangers of civil war are portrayed spectacularly in the third act of his first adaptation, when "The Scene is drawn, and there appears [*sic*] Houses and Towns burning, Men and Women hang'd upon Trees, and Children on the tops of Pikes."[3]

I Richard II

Tate's version of *Richard II* was cleverly adapted, but his choice of play was tactless. Even in Queen Elizabeth's day the deposition of Richard II was a sensitive subject: the queen and her contemporaries saw a parallel between the weak Richard II, who had no descendants, and Elizabeth, who would not name an heir and who was accused of being ruled by her favorites. Although Shakespeare's play was published three times during the queen's lifetime, one hundred and sixty-four lines in the fourth act containing the deposition scene were omitted each time; and the Lord Chamberlain's Men were questioned after they had performed the play on the eve of Essex's rebellion.[4]

The banning of Tate's play shows that a parallel was also easily found with the pleasure-loving and heirless Charles II. Indeed, at about the time the adaptation was performed, Sir Robert Howard, Dryden's brother-in-law and collaborator in *The Indian Queen*, and also a member of Parliament opposed to the exclusion policy, but favoring a Protestant succession, published anonymously his two-hundred-and-forty-page *Life and Reign of King Richard the Second*. Although Howard did not make his parallels explicit, he did emphasize and analyze the errors made by Richard that led to his downfall, including favoritism, and the king's struggling with and threatening to do without Parliament.[5] Tate seems to have played down these faults in presenting Richard, but whoever knew his English history knew the faults traditionally assigned to the last of the Plantagenets.

George Odell complains of the "note of disingenuousness" in Tate's six-page Epistle Dedicatory.[6] The adapter seems to have overstated his case because of his indignation:

> They that have not seen [the play] Acted, by its being silenc't, must suspect me to have Compil'd a Disloyal or Reflecting Play. But how far distant this was from my Design and Conduct in the Story will appear to him that reads with half

> an Eye. To form any Resemblance between the Times here written of, and the Present, had been unpardonable Presumption in Me. If the Prohibiters conceive any such Notion I am not accountable for That. I fell upon the new-modelling of this Tragedy, (as I had just before done on the *History of King Lear*) charm'd with the many Beauties I discover'd in it, which I knew wou'd become the Stage; with as little design of Satyr upon present Transactions, as Shakespear himself that wrote this Story before this Age began. I am not ignorant of the posture of Affairs in King Richard the Second's Reign, how dissolute then the Age, and how corrupt the Court; a Season that beheld Ignorance and Infamy preferr'd to Office and Pow'r, exercis'd in Oppressing, Learning and Merit; but why a History of those Times shou'd be supprest as a Libel upon Ours, is past my Understanding. . . .[7]

In what follows Tate emphasizes that he has made Richard more responsible and York and Gaunt more loyal than they were in the original. Later in the Epistle he says that he "expected [the adaptation] wou'd have found Protection from whence it receiv'd Prohibition" and that it probably would have if it had not been suppressed "without Examination."[8]

Actually, Tate included a little incidental satire on the court but considerably more satire against the Whigs. His denial that he is writing a "Disloyal" play or satirizing "present Transactions" is a denial to members of the court party that he is satirizing them, as he explains in the next sentence. Moreover, he felt that he had removed most of the anti-Tory satire by improving the behavior of his characters—and yet the authorities had not even troubled to look at his efforts, for they had suppressed the play without reading it. He does not *say* that he was satirizing the Whigs, because to admit that his satire had backfired would turn the joke on him; he can only speak of reading "with half an Eye" and "how far distant this was from my Design," with the broader hint that he had expected "Protection" for the play from those who prohibited it.

Tate's bitterness, then, is that of a playwright twice disappointed by the banning of his play, in which he was accused of doing the opposite of what he had intended to do by authorities who had not even read what he had written. Tate does not meet the objection to *Richard II* from a Tory politician's point of view, which is that, no matter how much the adapter may have put Richard's deposer in the wrong, the play still deals with a historical English precedent for the deposition of a king. Altering the title to *The Sicilian Usurper* and renaming some of the characters was not sufficient to meet such an objection. (Richard became Oswald, and new names were supplied for Gaunt, York, Bullingbrook, Northumberland, and the Queen; but Carlile, Aumarl, Exton, and others retained their names.)[9]

There are four major alterations made by Tate in his Richard II. The most important of these is the change in Richard himself, an alteration that Tate discussed at some length in his Dedicatory Epistle. Shakespeare, he complained, had made his characters no worse than history presented them but "never a jot better." Tate, on the other hand, went to some pains to elevate Richard's character and put the burden of deposition upon others: "I have every where given him the Language of an Active, Prudent Prince. Preferring the Good of his Subjects to his own private Pleasure. . . . My Design was to engage the pitty of the Audience for him in his Distresses, which I cou'd never have compass'd had I not before shewn him a Wise, Active and Just Prince."[10]

Although Bushy, Bagot, and Green are mentioned,[11] they do not appear in the play; and the influence of favorites upon Richard is barely touched upon. On the other hand, just before the deposition scene, York (still loyal to Richard), his Duchess, and Aumarl discuss the king, speaking of his heroic suppression of Wat Tyler's rebellion earlier in his reign and of his slaughter of the rebellious Irish Kernes. When Richard appears, he recounts the "curst Accident[s] i'th' power of Chance" that have led to his downfall. He resigns his crown because the only alternative is civil war; therefore, not lack of kingly resolve but love of his people leads him to give way:

> My gen'rous Friends, let Crowns and Scepters go
> Before I swim to 'em in Subjects blood.

The King in pity to his Subjects quits
His Right, that have no pity for their King![12]

Earlier, Richard has been absolved of most of the responsibility for the rebellion itself. Instead of his insolence to Gaunt in the deathbed scene, Tate has Richard apologize to his dying uncle for "the sallies of [his] youthful Blood" and receive Gaunt's apology for the scolding he has administered (which, since it emphasizes the "Ryot of [the] Court," would still be unwelcome to the king's friends). After Gaunt's death, Richard announces that he will borrow the revenues of Lancaster; and, when York objects that he is making a dangerous enemy of Bullingbrook, Richard replies: "Be Heav'n our judge we mean him nothing fowl / But shortly will with interest restore / The Loan our sudden streights make necessary."[13] Instead, then, of simply seizing Gaunt's revenues as Shakespeare's Richard does and thereby turning against himself the great noblemen of the kingdom, Tate's hero merely borrows; later, York confesses that he, as Gaunt's executor, had permitted the loan.[14]

Our sympathy for Richard is aroused, and his nobility is emphasized at the end of the play. In the prison scene he is presented as having been without food for three days. A table with a banquet then appears but "sinks down" when he attempts to eat. Comparing himself to Tantalus, he stoically accepts "what my Torturers please." After a romantic song is sung, he receives a letter from the Queen and expresses his love for her. When Exton and his companions enter, Richard "Kills 4 of them" (rather than Shakespeare's two).[15] The disappearing table had been a highly successful stage effect in the Restoration *Tempest,* but both this device and Richard's killing four of his attackers have support in such historians as Holinshed, whose *Chronicles* record alternative versions of Richard's end: "the common fame is, that he was everie daie served at the table with costlie meat, like a king, to the intent that no creature should suspect anie thing done contrarie to the order taken in the parlement; and when the meat was set before him, he was forbidden once to touch it; yea, he was not permitted so much as to smell to [*sic*] it, and so he died of forced famine."[16] Holinshed also records the story that, rather than starving to death, Richard was murdered by Exton and his companions, of whom he killed four. Tate's account is an ingenious combination of spectacle, historical detail, and heroic behavior.

The second principal change that Tate made in Shakespeare's play was the development of the role of the Queen. Not only does this alteration provide a larger part for an actress and develop the love interest that was expected in Restoration drama, but it also helps make Richard a more sympathetic figure. Although the Queen actually has fewer lines in the earlier part of the adaptation than she has in the original, she becomes a major figure after Richard has returned from Ireland. In Tate's version, she and the Duchess of York meet Richard on the "Heath" immediately after his landing. Also, just before the deposition scene, the Queen enters "supported by Ladies" and speaks fifty-one lines in a conversation with the Duchess of York and Richard. Later, she meets Richard on his way to banishment (as in Shakespeare), but the dialogue is largely rewritten.[17] The language the lovers speak, when it is not from Shakespeare, is in the artificial Restoration vein of Edgar and Cordelia. However, the scenes are wisely placed; and, as Odell remarks of them, "whatever we may think of their stilted verse, [they are] not despicable as acting *media*. Under the tinsel, some real feeling is discernible."[18]

The third important change occurs in the character and behavior of the Duke of York, in whom Tate seems to have tried to combine several incompatible qualities. First, York is a mouthpiece for sentiments of loyalty: in Act I, Scene ii, for example, after the Duchess of Gloucester has urged Gaunt to avenge Gloucester's death by killing Richard, and Gaunt has refused (much as in Shakespeare), York enters to drive the lesson home. After telling the duchess that her "very Tears are Treason," he and his brother walk out on their widowed sister-in-law.[19] But, in Act II, Scene i, the mouthpiece of loyalty becomes also a satirist of the court and—despite Tate's protest to the contrary—of Charles II's court. Here York is at first loyal in criticizing Gaunt's son, but then he describes the general political situation in pointed terms: "Villany takes its time, all goes worse and worse in Ireland, Rebellion is there on the Wing, and here in the Egg; yet still the Court dances after the French Pipe, Eternal Apes of Vanity: Mutiny stirring, Discipline asleep, Knaves in Office, all's wrong; make much of your Sickness Brother: if it be Mortal, 'tis worth a Dukedome."[20] At the same time, the duke is fat and often obviously comic—characteristics that might be considered uncomplimentary to the other Duke of York, Charles II's brother.

The fourth major alteration is in the attitude toward Bullingbrook. Shakespeare's Bolingbroke is an ambiguous figure whose intentions are not apparent until the fourth act; but Tate's leaves nothing to doubt. At the end of the first act, as he goes into banishment, Bullingbrook makes clear his designs:

> ... I feel my veins work high,
> And conscious glory kindling in my brest,
> Inspires a Thought to vast to be exprest;
> Where this disgrace will end the Heav'ns can tell,
> And Her'ford's Soul divines, that 'twill be well!
> A Beam of royal splendor strikes my Eye,
> Before my charm'd sight, Crowns and Scepters fly;
> The minutes big with Fate, too slowly run,
> But hasty Bullingbrook shall push 'em on.[21]

After this clear exposition of Bullingbrook's ambition and after Richard has only "borrowed" Gaunt's revenues with York's permission, there is hardly anything to be said for the rebels' cause. Moreover, when Richard's coffin is brought in at the end of the play, Bullingbrook is even more repentant in Tate than in Shakespeare: "In vain I wish The happy Change cou'd be, / That I slept There, and Richard Mourn'd for Me."[22]

Tate's most substantial addition to the play is a new scene in Act II, which brings Bullingbrook together with a rabble whom the adapter doubtless intended for Whigs: "Enter Rabble] A Shoomaker, Farrier, Weaver, Tanner, Mercer. [*sic*] Brewer, Butcher, Barber, and infinite others with a Confused Noise."[23] The mob's leader, Revelation Stitch, who boasts that he had been a follower of Wat Tyler and Jack Straw, is anxious "to kill all the Nobility and Clergy." The rabble are supposed to decide whether they will support Bullingbrook but are soon scuffling among themselves over whether or not their Commonwealth should have laws.

When Bullingbrook arrives, he proclaims that he does not intend to usurp the throne; but when he discovers that the mob wants him to do so, he smoothly reverses himself and announces that he will not "usurp" but will take the throne in order to dispense justice and win victories. As his first act, he orders that Revelation Stitch be hanged. The people comprising the mob vacillate in the interests of satire: first they agree that, since their leader had been "a false Prophet" in not foreseeing his own death, he must hang; then they are ready to defend him; but, when Bullingbrook threatens to use his army, they agree to "Let justice have it's course."[24] As for the inclusion of such comedy in his tragedy, Tate explained in his Epistle that it was "necessary to help off the heaviness of the Tale," and he again quoted Dryden's Epistle Dedicatory to *The Spanish Friar* in his support.[25]

The alterations of Tate are, then, intelligently made in view of the purpose he wished to achieve: to dress up a politically relevant play with anti-Whig satire and other topical comment and to make it entertaining theater fare. Richard is made a more sympathetic figure and is relieved almost entirely of responsibility for his fate; all sympathy for Bullingbrook is removed, and he becomes a guilty and, finally, a repentant usurper. The mob scene is amusing, and the love scenes arouse pity for Richard and his queen. The principal flaw in this plan was that the play itself was unalterably anti-Tory in its essentials, and an anti-Whig veneer was insufficient to cover them. Tate's unpolitical mind failed to grasp the danger in the story of Richard II, no matter how it was told—the danger of a successful deposition.

II The Ingratitude of a Common-Wealth

The political conflict reached a climax in March, 1681, when the king summoned Parliament to meet at Oxford. Heretofore, he had needed it in order to raise money; but this time, while Parliament was meeting at Oxford, he concluded a secret agreement with Louis XIV which brought him sufficient income to dispense with its aid. Even as the House of Commons again considered the matter of exclusion, therefore, it was dismissed; and it was not again convened during the four years that remained of Charles's rule. The Tories had triumphed, and by summer Charles was strong enough to move against his enemies. In July, Shaftesbury, charged with high treason, was sent to the Tower of London; and although the Whig grand jury released him at his trial in November, popular opinion in the country as a whole was running in the king's favor. About November 17, a week before Shaftesbury's trial, Dryden's *Absalom and Achitophel* was published; Tate's adaptation of *Coriolanus* was first performed in December or January.[26]

Richard II may have been condemned unread merely on the basis of its dangerous subject, but this time Tate's title showed the anti-Whig position clearly. He was equally explicit in his Dedication:

> Upon a close view of this Story, there appear'd in some Passages, no small Resemblance with the busie Faction of our own time. And I confess, I chose rather to set the Parallel nearer to Sight, than to throw it off at a further Distance. Yet there are none that can apply any Part (as Satyr) on themselves, whose Designs and Practises are not of the same Cast. What offence to any good Subject in Stygmatizing on the Stage those Troublers of the State, that out of private Interest or Mallice, Seduce the Multitude to Ingratitude, against Persons that are not only plac't in Rightful Power above them; but also the Heroes and Defenders of their Country.
>
> Where is the harm of letting the People see what Miseries Common-Wealths have been involv'd in, by a blind Compliance with their popular Misleaders: . . . Faction is a Monster that often makes the slaughter 'twas designed for; and as often turns its fury on those that hacht it. The Moral therefore of these Scenes being to Recommend Submission and Adherence to Establisht Lawful Power, which in a word, is LOYALTY.[27]

Except for considerable cutting of lines, speeches, and some of the shorter scenes, Tate's first four acts are not greatly different from Shakespeare's. But the arrangement of scenes shows a tightening of the action and an adjustment to a theater in which a change of place meant a change of scenery. In Act I, editors of Shakespeare's *Coriolanus* since the eighteenth century have provided ten scenes in ten different locations: (1) Rome. A street; (2) Corioli. The Senate House; (3) Rome. A room in Marcius' house; (4) Before Corioli; (5) Within Corioli. A street; (6) Near the camp of Cominius; (7) The gates of Corioli; (8) A field of battle between the Roman and the Volscian camps; (9) The Roman camp; and (10) The camp of the Volsces.[28] Of these, Tate simply omitted the contents of four scenes: 2, 6, 7, and 10. His first scene is headed "The City Rome"; the second is "A Palace"; the third, which is "before the Walls of Corioles," contains parts of Shakespeare's scenes 4 and 5; and the fourth, which begins "Scene Changes to a Camp or Field," contains parts of scenes 8 and 9. Tate's second act has no location but is presumably "The City Rome" again. Then "Scene opening, shews the Senate sitting in the Capitol; Coriolanus in a White Robe, as Candidate for the Consulship"; this is followed by "Scene the Street." This scene apparently continues throughout the next act: it is where the fight with the people takes place, where Coriolanus meets his mother (Shakespeare's III, ii), and where Coriolanus is banished and parts with his family (Shakespeare's III, iii and IV, i).

In Act IV Tate omits the second and third scenes in Shakespeare (the Tribunes meeting the women, and the Roman and Volsce meeting on the highway). Instead, he begins with Coriolanus in front of Aufidius's house; then shutters representing the front of the house are drawn back, and the audience sees "The Inside of the Palace; Musick Plays; Servants pass hastily over the Stage." The ensuing encounter of Aufidius and Coriolanus is combined with Aufidius's revelation of his intentions (Shakespeare's v and vii). We return to Rome (Shakespeare's vi) and, following that, see an elaborate tableau stressing the dangers of civil war: "Scene Opening, shews

Coriolanus seated in State, in a rich Pavilion, his Guards and Soudiers with lighted Torches, as ready to set Fire on [*sic*] Rome; Petitioners as from the Citty offer him Papers, which he scornfully throws by: At length Menenius comes forward, and speaks to him: Aufidius with Nigridius, making Remarks on 'em."[29] After the failure of Menenius's appeal (Shakespeare's V, ii), and as the trumpets are sounded and the soldiers advance with their torches to burn the city, Volumnia, Virgilia, and Young Martius arrive with their plea. Their success ends Act IV.

The play, then, made use of the spectacular effects and striking "discoveries" that were possible with movable shutters at the same time as it avoided unnecessary scene changes and made the action swifter and more concentrated. Evidently, Tate felt that the moral was plain enough, for Coriolanus still scolds and does much—more than Richard II—to bring about his own downfall. The mob is guilty of almost destroying the country; and, in Tate, the mob's leaders, the Tribunes, are dragged off by their followers to execution. However, Tate did provide Coriolanus with a new speech to the Tribunes in Act III, Scene i, which emphasizes the play's political import. Having addressed them as "Spawn of Sedition, and the Spawners of it," Coriolanus continues:

> You, Faction-Mongers,
> That wear your formal Beards, and Plotting Heads,
> By the Valour of the Men you Persecute;
> Canting Caballers, that in smoaky Cells,
> Amongst Crop-ear'd Mechanicks, wast the Night
> In Villanous Harrangues against the State.
> There may Your Worship's Pride be seen t'embrace
> A smutty Tinker, and in extasy
> Of Treason, shake a Cobler be th' wax't Thumb.[30]

The character of Coriolanus is not much altered, but the Restoration practice of cutting and simplifying the longer speeches reduces his heroic stature as it did Lear's.

Tate's adaptation anticipated Dr. Johnson's observation that the first act of *Coriolanus* had "too much bustle" in it and the last "too little."[31] In Shakespeare, only the hero dies, but in Tate the stage is covered with blood. At the beginning of Act V, after the ladies have been welcomed in Rome, they receive news that Nigridius (a new character who resents earlier maltreatment by Coriolanus) is plotting against the hero in Corioles. They return with Young Martius, and it is at Corioles that the bloody climax takes place. After we have seen the plotters and learned that Aufidius lusts for Virgilia, the scene moves to the Palace, where, before the Lords of Corioles, Coriolanus is wounded by Aufidius and the Conspirators, though he "kills some, and hurts Aufidius." To a background of fighting between the troops of the two leaders, Virgilia is brought in to satisfy the lust of Aufidius; but, in the Roman tradition, she has stabbed herself. Aufidius dies of his wound; Virgilia and Coriolanus part; and she dies. Nigridius gloats, boasting that he has killed Menenius and has tortured Young Martius. Then "Enter Volumnia Distracted, with Young Martius under her Arm"; she raves and "Snatches a Partizan from the foremost of the Guards, and strikes Nigridius through, as she runs off." Coriolanus and Young Martius say their farewells and die.

The hero, wounded first but dying last, resembles Theocrin in *The Loyal General*, as indeed the huddled series of deaths are reminiscent of the conclusion of the earlier play. Both are melodramatic and sentimental in their emphasis on the parting of dying lovers or of members of a family. This conclusion also owes a debt to *King Lear*, for Tate, who had admired Poor Tom's mad language, imitated it in Volumnia's ravings:

> Ha! What a merry World is this Elizium!
> See how the youthful Sheepherds trip to the Pipe,
> And fat Silenus waddles in the Round.
> Beware thy Horns, Pan, Cupid's with their Bow-strings
> Have ty'd 'em fast to th' Tree! Ah, ha! ha! ha!
> Whats that?—a Summons to me from the Gods?
> Back Mercury, and tell 'em I'll appear.[32]

Unlike Poor Tom, who imagines a Christian hell, Volumnia thinks she is in the Classical underworld.

The role of Nigridius is increased over that of the nameless lieutenant in Shakespeare's play who advises Aufidius, partly to help bring about the gruesome ending and partly to help support the hero's character by emphasizing the evil motives of his enemies. The character whose role is most enlarged, however, is Valeria, who is described in the cast as "An affected, talkative, fantastical Lady" and at her first appearance as "Gawdily and Fantastically Drest, follow'd by Six or Seven Pages." She acts up to her role of the talkative, empty-headed belle: "And do I look Sovereignly Madam? Indeed I think my Enemies will Grant me That; but I bear not upon't: I am Ambitious only of the Graces of the Mind, the Intellectuals, and despise those vain Allurements of Dress and Face—but do I look Sovereignly Madam?"[33] She speaks forty-four of the fifty-one lines remaining in the scene after her appearance, and the seven speeches that are delivered by others are one line each. She also dominates the other two scenes in which she appears, and Tate finds cause to dismiss her or simply does not introduce her when there is business to be accomplished; but she survives to speak the Epilogue. Although Valeria seems out of place in Republican Rome, she is an amusing character in herself; and her absurdity adds to the comedy of Shakespeare's drama (which was enough to prompt Dr. Johnson's other famous observation about *Coriolanus*—that it is "one of the most amusing" of Shakespeare's dramas).[34]

Many of Shakespeare's plays, including *Richard II* and *Coriolanus*, seem to present issues about which there is much to say for both sides and to resolve themselves as stories without supporting either side. Many Jacobean tragedies also handle issues in this way, and Restoration drama is sometimes almost capable of it. But when the drama becomes political, it loses its objectivity. Both *Richard II* and *Coriolanus* suffer from this narrowing: the rightness of the cause of the title characters far outweighs any errors they may have committed, and their opponents are simply wrong.

In Tate's three adaptations of Shakespeare—but especially in the first and third—he directed his efforts to improving probability, clarity, swift movement, coherence, and stage effectiveness for the theater of his day; but he largely ignored poetic justice (in the success of Bullingbrook and the fate of Coriolanus's family), the unities, and the Neoclassical canon that comedy should be omitted in tragedy. In all his dedications, Tate had high praise for Shakespeare. Even in the eager bitterness of his Epistle to Raynsford he excused publishing his redaction of *Richard II* on the grounds that "it still retains the immortal Spirit of its first-Father"; and in the Dedication of *The Ingratitude,* addressed to Lord Herbert, he was glad to have "Launcht out in Shakespear's Bottom. Much of what is offered here, is Fruit that grew in the Richness of his Soil; and what ever the Superstructure prove, it was my good fortune to build upon a Rock."[35]

III The Second Part of Absalom and Achitophel

The Second Part of Absalom and Achitophel was published about November 10, 1682, almost a year after the first part.[36] Much had happened during that year. After Shaftesbury had been released, he had taken the lead in planning an insurrection. When the Duke of Monmouth was deposed as chancellor of Cambridge in April, he too began to talk of rebellion; he toured the western part of England in September, hoping to increase his popularity. It was planned that a rising would take place on his return to London, but he was arrested, and a warrant was also issued for Shaftesbury's arrest. Although new plans were made after Monmouth was set free on bail, Shaftesbury, who had been in hiding, fled to Holland in the month that the *Second Part* appeared.

Meanwhile, the Tories had other successes. In March, 1682, James returned from his seventeen-month exile in Scotland. When he went north in May to bring back his duchess, his ship was wrecked; but he escaped and returned to London on May 27, where he soon exerted considerable influence on the king. In the summer, the court party achieved victory in the London elections when a Tory lord mayor and two Tory sheriffs were chosen; it is with this Tory victory that the poem ends. Two years later, when Tate looked back on the events of 1678-82 in a dedication to James's daughter, Princess Anne, he remarked that "so raging was that Season of Faction, that no Son of Loyalty could want Indignation enough to constitute a Poet."[37]

The Second Part of Absalom and Achitophel is weaker than its predecessor for several reasons. One, of course, is a difference in the quality of the poets, Dryden and Tate. But Dryden himself could not have written a second part that would have rivaled the first. The temptation of Monmouth and the conflict between Shaftesbury and Charles, which were central in the earlier poem, were much more dramatic than the return of the Duke of York from exile, which is the climax of the *Second Part.* And the brilliant relevance of the biblical parallel in the original poem did not extend to the events that Tate had to celebrate: if the assignment had not been to write a sequel, there would have been little point in choosing the biblical parallel at all.

The poem also suffers from the accidents of history. With the climax as James's return, the ethical center of the *Second Part* is the rightness of the country's submission to order and law as represented by James's retaining his rights of succession; and the poem includes high praise of James as symbol and as man. From our vantage point in history, we are likely to make only grudging allowance for praise of the symbol and none at all for praise of the man; and we may accuse Tate of time-serving. However, he simply praises the Duke of York for virtues that contemporaries thought he had: he was still known as the brave admiral responsible for the victory of Lowestoft (1665) and for vigorous action at Sole Bay (1672); he was not yet recognized as the coward who fled from England upon William's arrival and from Ireland after the Battle of the Boyne. Moreover, his religious bigotry was not yet apparent to Englishmen. Most of all, he was loved by the court party as one loves the man he has fought for, the tangible symbol of the political principles in which he believes and the victories to which he has contributed. To many Englishmen besides Tate, the duke represented order and tradition.

Indeed, Tate's portrait of James was a fairly accurate one, judging by other comments of contemporaries. For example, after quoting a contemporary as saying that James "in his conversation and arguing . . . endeavoured rather to convince with good reason than fine expressions," that he was "all his life, a great enemy to drinking, gaming and all such pleasures as were obstructive to business . . . or were but loss of time, which he always accounted precious," and that "he was a kind husband" and "the most indulgent father in the world," a distinguished modern historian remarks that, "in contemporary correspondence, a constantly reiterated theme [was] the contrast between the virtue and reliability of James and the fickleness and debauchery of his brother; indeed, if high purpose, consistency, and industry ensure success in the art of governing, then the new king had all the qualifications for a brilliant reign."[38] Tate's portrait of James seems to have been drawn from the same point of view:

> Ev'n in the worst of men the noblest parts
> Confess him, and he triumphs in their hearts,
> Whom to his king the best respects commend
> Of subject, soldier, kinsman, prince, and friend;
> All sacred names of most divine esteem,
> And to perfection all sustain'd by him,
> Wise, just, and constant, courtly without art,
> Swift to discern and to reward desert;
> No hour of his in fruitless ease destroy'd,
> But on the noblest subjects still employ'd;
> Whose steady soul ne'er learnt to separate
> Between his monarch's int'rest and the State,
> But heaps those blessings on the royal head,
> Which he well knows must be on subjects shed. (ll. 633-46)[39]

Tate's lines do not express the verdict of history but they make articulate the feeling of many at this time, and they make their point with enthusiasm. Tate belittles the dangers of a Catholic king: the people would never accept the Catholic Church because, Tate remarks ironically, the Jews (Englishmen) know that they might be required to surrender their lands again and "they grutch God's tythes" (1. 661). Moreover, Tate argues—naively, in view of later events—that James would have no means of imposing a change in the national church; certainly, Parliament would not help him. Louis XIV wants disunity in England, says Tate, and would not come to James's aid—and this topic leads the poet to point out the dangers of civil war.

David (who represents Charles II) then asserts himself, announcing that "Succession [is] fix'd by Heav'n, the kingdom's bar, / Which once dissolv'd, admits the flood of war" (11. 773-74); and James returns, to the delight of his followers. After the latter have been listed, we have an account of the shipwreck (a Tory account, for James's enemies accused him of saving his belongings at the expense of human lives), which calls for reflections on the "toil of fate" that is necessary to "build a man of fame," a hero (1. 1115). Finally, we see the triumphant return of the "royal lovers" (1. 1127) to London and are told in a brief epilogue of the court party's victory in the London elections.

The pattern of Tate's poem follows very closely the pattern of its predecessor, for seven of the eight parts into which the earlier poem may be divided have parallels in the second:

(1) Introduction *(Absalom and Achitophel,* 11. 1-149; *Second Part,* 11. 1-114).
(2) Portrait of Achitophel *(AA,* 11. 150-229; nothing corresponding in *SP).*
(3) Temptation of Absalom *(AA,* 11. 230-476; *SP,* 11. 115-275).
(4) Achitophel's Followers *(AA,* 11. 477-681; *SP,* 11. 276-555, 11. 310-509 by Dryden).
(5) Actions and Reflections on the Actions of Absalom *(AA,* 11. 682-810) and the Prince (*SP,* 11. 556-930).
(6) David's Follower's (*AA,* 11. 811-932; *SP,* 11. 931-1064).
(7) David's Speech (*AA,* 11. 933-1024, corresponiding to the Prince's return, *SP,* 11. 1065-1130).
(8) Conclusion (*AA,* 11. 1025-31; *SP,* 11. 1131-40).

Other parallel elements include a decisive speech by David in the *Second Part* (11. 733-90), moved to an earlier position where it accompanies the departure of James, and a catalogue of *types* of rebels in the *Second Part* (11. 97-114) like that in the earlier poem (11. 495-542). The *Second Part* also imitates or borrows a few lines from the first part.[40]

Like Dryden, Tate uses suggestions of the epic—with occasional reference to *Paradise Lost*—to confer dignity upon his subject and to imply parallels.[41] The epic is suggested by such conventional means as the elevated style, catalogues of heroes on both sides, long speeches by major figures, and epic similes (11. 558-65, 833-40, 919-26). *Paradise Lost* is suggested by such phrases as "To this Hell's agent" (1. 240) in introducing Achitophel, who is about to reply to Absalom; and by Tate's invocation of the "lab'ring Muse" (1. 935) with the exclamation "Hard task! yet will not I thy flight recall" (1. 939), a line reminiscent of Milton's "Sad task, yet argument / Not less but more heroic" *(Paradise Lost*, IX, 13-14). Milton is also suggested in Tate's comparison of the first part of *Absalom and Achitophel* with *Paradise Lost*. The parallel is implied in the portrait of Dryden as Asaph:

> How fierce his satire loos'd; restrain'd, how tame;
> How tender of th' offending young man's fame!
> How well his worth, and brave adventures styl'd;
> Just to his virtues, to his error mild.
> No page of thine that fears the strictest view,
> But teems with just reproof, or praise as due;
> Not Eden could a fairer prospect yield,
> All paradise without one barren field:
> Whose wish the censure of his foes has pass'd;
> The song of Asaph shall for ever last! (11. 1049-58).

The last line is a refrain used three times (1042, 1047, 1058) and then varied to "The Song of Asaph and the fame shall last" (1064). "Asaph" is the name of one of David's chief musicians of the Temple, and in 2 Chron. 20: 14-23 a "son of Asaph" by his inspired song raises Judah to victory over the rebellious Edomites. The *Second Part* is more literary in its concerns: not only are Dryden's well-known portraits of Settle and Shadwell as Doeg and Og (11. 412-509) concerned with writers, but Dryden also contributed an extended comment on Ben-Jochanan (Reverend Samuel Johnson) in 11. 350-95; and Tate praised not only Dryden himself but also Sir Roger L'Estrange, the licenser of the press (11. 1025-36) under the name of Sheva, a Scribe of King David's (2 Sam. 20: 25).

Tonson reported in 1716 that Dryden had written two

hundred lines of the poem (11. 310-509), "besides some touches in other places." Sir Walter Scott, however, claimed for Dryden "much of" the portrait of Corah (11. 79-94) and the descriptions of the Green-Ribbon Club and Arod (11. 522-55). He contrasted these with Tate's portraits of the Queen as Michal (11. 51-68) and of Asaph, both of which he described as "flat, common-place, and uninteresting."[42] However, the portrait of Michal seems to be drawn with a deliberate attempt at gentleness and sympathy for the outrageously treated Queen; and it is immediately followed by the portrait of Corah, the wicked accuser, portrayed with more indignation because of the defenselessness of the Queen, his victim. The change in vigor does not necessarily mean a change in authorship. Similarly, the portrait of Asaph has a deliberately lyric quality and is different from most of the rest of the poem in this respect. The portrait of Rabsheka (11. 298-309) shows that Tate had the ability to write strong, clever satire. In this poem, he had not only Dryden's advice but also the model of the first part to follow; under these conditions, he might well write with more vigor than usual and successfully imitate the style of his collaborator.

CHAPTER 6

Farce and Jacobean Drama

THE REPUTATION of farce was low during the Restoration period, when both the name and the thing appeared to be new. The term "farce" had been used only rarely with reference to the theater before 1660;[1] and, although Elizabethan and Jacobean dramatists had employed farcical elements in their plays, they had seldom written farces as such. But after the Restoration, the name was applied to "various kinds of stage-piece emphasizing ridiculous action rather than nature and probability," including *Commedia dell'arte,* Duffett's burlesques of Shakespearean "opera," and "drolls" (cut version of plays emphasizing broad comedy).[2] The newness of the term, which implied that this kind of play was newer than it was, encouraged hostility and critical disapproval. Dramatists who preferred to write more traditional and, they felt, more worthwhile kinds of comedy, objected because farces were often highly successful in the theater; and since the chief example for writing plays of this kind seemed to come from abroad, farces were especially scorned by native critics.

Shadwell and Edward Howard were among the dramatists who recorded their dislike of farce; but the objections that probably meant the most to Tate were those of Dryden, who complained about farce in several of his writings, including the Prologue he wrote for Tate's *Loyal General,* in which he protested against the audience's preference for "nonsense" over "strong wit": "Therefore thin nourishment of farce ye choose, / Decoctions of a barley-water Muse." Dryden attempted to distinguish between farce and comedy in his preface to *An Evening's Love* (1671):

> But I have descended, before I was aware, from Comedy to Farce; which consists principally of grimaces. That I admire not any comedy equally with tragedy, is, perhaps, from the sullenness of my humor; but that I detest those farces, which are now the most frequent entertainments of the stage, I am sure I have reason on my side. Comedy consists, though of low persons, yet of natural actions and characters; I mean such humours, adventures, and designs, as are to be found and met with in the world. Farce, on the other side, consists of forced humours, and unnatural events. Comedy presents us with the imperfections of human nature: Farce entertains us with what is monstrous and chimerical. The one causes laughter in those who can judge of men and manners, by the lively representation of their folly or corruption: the other produces the same effect in those who can judge of neither, and that only by its extravagances. The first works on the judgement and fancy; the latter on the fancy only: there is more of satisfaction in the former kind of laughter, and in the latter more of scorn. But, how it happens, that an impossible adventure should cause our mirth, I cannot so easily imagine.[3]

In 1692 the newly appointed laureate's farce *A Duke and No Duke* was still "being often acted,"[4] and Tate may have felt obliged to reply to Dryden's new complaint about the popularity of farce in the Preface to *Cleomenes* (1692), which included the provacative remark that "Were I in the humour, I have sufficient cause to expose [Farce] in its true colours; but . . . I will forbear my satire."[5] Early in 1693, Tate wrote a dedicatory preface for the Earl of Orrery's hitherto unpublished farcical comedy *Guzman*.[6] Then he republished *A Duke and No Duke* with a substantial new Preface defending farce.

I *The Defense of Farce*

Performed initially in August, 1684, *A Duke and No Duke* had been played before royalty on November 3 and again on December 9. It was quickly published with a brief Preface attributing its success to the royal favor.[7] In the rosy glow of royal approval, Tate boasted that he had made the events in the play more natural and probable than they had been in his source and that, since writing farce is harder than writing comedy, a successful farce is especially deserving of admiration.

Eight years later, this mild defense was insufficient. The expanded Preface of 1693 begins with the typically modest hope that it may "provoke some Learned Person" to write a better defense of farce than this one. Concerned to find authority to support the dignity of farce, Tate found some assistance in Agesilao Mariscotti's (1577-1618) Latin treatise about the use of masks by the ancients, which had been published in 1610 and reprinted in 1639 and 1691. Although Mariscotti was concerned with the carnival at Venice rather than with farce, Tate gives an abstract of part of the Italian writer's work to show that masks were widely used in Classical times.[8] Then Tate argues that, since masks lend themselves naturally to farcical action, Classical drama must have included farce. After additional citations from Classical authorities, Tate concludes that "'tis plain that both the Greeks and Romans had Farcical Plays."[9] To a modern reader, this part of the argument seems too long and not a very compelling defense of the genre; and he wishes that Tate would distinguish more clearly between plays that are wholly farce and plays that merely include some farcical action.

Next, Tate turns to specific examples of the use of farce. The plays of Aristophanes and Plautus are largely farce, he argues; and he also mentions Shakespeare's *Comedy of Errors*, Fletcher's (modern scholarship says Beaumont's) *Knight of the Burning Pestle*, Jonson's *Alchemist* ("Farce from the opening of the First Scene to the end of the Intreigue [*sic*]")[10] and *Volpone* (the mountebank scene and Sir Politic's hiding himself under a tortoise shell), and *The Rehearsal*. Tate concludes by quietly pointing out that Dryden also has written farce in *Sir Martin Mar-All* (from Moliere's *L'Etourdi*) and in the last scene of *The Spanish Friar*.

But what is farce? Although Tate hesitates to define it, he does say something about it as opposed to comedy:

> . . . Comedy properly so called, is an Imitation of Humane Life, . . . and subsists upon Nature; so that whosoever has a Genius to coppy her, and will take the Pains, is assured of Success, and all the World affords him Subject. Whereas the

> business of Farce extends beyond Nature and Probability. But then there are so few Improbabilities that will appear pleasant in the Representation, that it will strain the best Invention to find them out, and require the nicest Judgment to manage them when they are conceived. Extravagant and monstrous Fancies are but sick Dreams, that rather torment than divert the Mind; but when Extravagancy and Improbability happen to please at all, they do it to purpose, because they strike our Thought with greatest Surprise. . . .
>
> . . . Comedy may admit of Humour, which is a great Province of Farce; but then it might be such Humor as comes within compass of Nature and Probability: For where it exceeds these Bounds it becomes Farce. Which Freedom I would allow a Poet, and thank him into the Bargain, provided he has the Judgment so to manage his Excursion, as to heighten my Mirth without too grosly shocking my Senses.[11]

Farce, then, consists of restrained improbabilities, hard to find and hard to manage, but pleasing because they surprise.

Later critics have not found farce easy to define. Leo Hughes, who devotes the first chapter of his *A Century of English Farce* to surveying definitions, concludes that "the chief, even the exclusive, business of farce is to stimulate the risibilities of the audience. The distinction between farce and other kinds of comic drama must then rest upon the nature of the laughter elicited by each." Comedy delineates "the play of character upon character"; burlesque, on the other hand, brings laughter "by imitation with intent to ridicule"; but farce "excite[s] laughter by ridiculous situations and incidents."[12] Rather than distinguishing on the basis of the kind of laughter involved, J. H. Wilson describes farce as "dominantly physical comedy. It deals in absurd and exaggerated situations, implausible complications, cheatings, cuckoldry, slapstick, and horseplay. Burlesque is farce which reduces a higher, or more serious, kind of drama to the lowest possible terms. Intrigue comedy, closely related to farce, lacks the roughness of slapstick and places more emphasis upon the ingenious manipulation of characters, situations, disguises, and misunderstandings in one or more sex intrigues, which usually end in marriage."[13]

Alvin Kernan, observing that farce is "quite closely related to parody and burlesque," suggests that it may be "understood as a dramatic technique that permits the author to show, without concern for realism, human foolishness and ineffectiveness."[14] Eric Bentley has suggested that farce, like melodrama, imitates not the surfaces of life (as does more naturalistic drama) but what is beneath the surface: "like dreams, farces show the disguised fulfillment of repressed wishes"[15]—an explanation which recalls Tate's remark that "Extravagant and monstrous Fancies are but sick Dreams" and that farce should avoid them. Tate's king-for-a-day drama, which one enters and leaves through magic (a frame within which all things become "possible") and which leads the characters from a universally unhappy and frustrating situation to a universally happy and satisfying solution, fits all these explanations of farce, including Bentley's.

II A Duke and No Duke

The source of *A Duke and No Duke* was *Trappolin Creduto Principe: or, Trappolin Supposed a Prince An Italian Trage-Comedy* by Aston Cokain (1608-83), an acquaintance of Sir John Suckling and others of the Tribe of Ben. We do not know whether his play had been performed before the closing of the theaters in 1642 or, indeed, whether it was performed after 1660;[16] but it had been published in 1658 with Cokain's poems and had been reissued in 1662 and 1669. However, *Trappolin* is of special interest to the historian of the drama since it is one of the very few English plays of its era in which there is an acknowledged debt to the *Commedia dell' arte*. Cokain, who spent a year in France and Italy (1632-33), said that he wrote *Trappolin* in Rome, Naples, and Paris after watching the original in Venice. Furthermore, he says that, because he only saw his source performed twice, his play is "no translation," which seems to imply that, though he has not attempted to use the words of his source, he has followed the plot fairly closely. Kathleen Lea found nine *scenarii* of the *Commedia* that are similar to *Trappolin* but none is an exact duplicate.[17]

Cokain relates the story of the gay Trappolin, who is transformed by magic to look like the Duke, thereby causing and participating in a series of farcical confusions. Restored at the end of the play by the magician (who, it turns out, is his father), he is forgiven by his mistress Flametta and by the Duke. In Cokain's drama, two other love plots also wind their way to an equally happy conclusion. Tate streamlines his source: the 28 characters, 5 acts, 15 scenes, and 2807 lines in Cokain are condensed to 15 characters, 3 acts, 9 scenes, and 1326 lines in Tate.[18] Tate omits the masque at the marriage of the Duke, the beginning of the secondary love affair between Brunetto and the Duke's sister Prudencia, and the whole of the other love affairs. He adds a scene between Trappolin and the foreign ambassadors and a conversation between Trappolin and Prudentia. The hero is modified from the gay, carefree Trappolin of Cokain's version to the "Parasite, Pimp, Fidler, and Buffoon" of Tate;[19] Flametta, too, endures a Restoration metamorphosis as a more worldly-wise but rather prudish heroine. Leo Hughes and A. H. Scouten remark that "the admitted gain in realism is offset by the loss of affection for" Trappolin;[20] but Tate was not primarily interested in affection for his hero.

Like most farces, *A Duke and No Duke* depends on disguise and mistaken identity which lead to a climax of confusion: the pace must be controlled, and something must be left for the climax. Tate arranges his material well. The first act is devoted to setting up the situation—the departure of the Duke to marry and bring home his bride; the transformation of Trappolin; his imprisonment of the Duke's advisers, Barbarino and Alberto; and his freeing of the Duke's enemy and Prudentia's lover, Brunetto. Of the two scenes in Act II, the first shows Trappolin dispensing "justice" to the Duke's subjects; and, in the second, the Duke returns with his bride, Isabella. The sequence of events is then rather mechanical but well paced: the Duke is increasingly dismayed as he hears of "his" actions, first from his advisers, and second from the lovers Brunetto and Prudentia. Next Trappolin meets, first, the lovers; second, the advisers; and, third, the new Duchess. Then (Act III, Scene i) the pattern is nearly repeated as the Duke meets the advisers, the Duchess, and the lovers; again Trappolin meets the advisers—and then the foreign ambassadors arrive. Confusions reach their climax in the last scene: after a signet belonging to the real Duke is returned to Trappolin and the two "Dukes" meet, Trappolin throws a powder in the Duke's face which transforms him so that he looks like Trappolin; the true Duke is then welcomed by Flammetta, maltreated by the advisers, and rejected by his bride and his sister—all before he is given a mirror so that he can see what he looks like. He is about to be locked up as incorrigible when the magician appears and resolves all misunderstandings quickly and happily.

Tate's version of the scene in which Trappolin dispenses justice is cleverly adapted. In Cokain's play, the three examples of Trappolin's dispensation of justice (IV, i) are as follows: first, a Puritan whose servant was killed by a drunken butcher is given permission to become drunk and kill the butcher; second, a man whose son was killed by a workman's falling off the roof on him is ordered to retaliate by falling off the roof on the murderer; and third, the coachman who has killed a widow's son is punished by being ordered to beget another son with the widow. In Tate (II, i), the first makes comic capital out of the double standard: Trappolin punishes the man who has debauched the widow's daughter by ordering the widow to debauch the man's son. The second, borrowed from Cokain, is that of the baby killed by a coachman, who is ordered to beget a replacement. Tate's third combines Cokain's first two ingeniously: the Puritan—caricatured as wearing "five Cassocks or Coats, seven Cloaks, and one dozen of quilted Caps" and as speaking an affected language—has been fallen upon by a workman who was working on "a new Mansion that [the Puritan] had prepared unto" himself, and the Puritan is ordered to fall off the top of his house on the workman in revenge.[21] The Puritan himself is an object of satire (though it is less coarse than that in Cokain's play), and the mansion and the falling workman seem to parody both the Puritan's concern with salvation and the inspiration he claimed to receive from heaven.

The play also contains dramatic burlesque. The title parodies that of Beaumont and Fletcher's *A King and No King.* [22] And

Mago the magician resembles Prospero in *The Tempest*: like Prospero, he has controlled the action of the play through magic, and he explains at the end that he is the banished Duke of Tuscany who has studied magic for twelve years "and in just Revenge / Have rais'd these strange disorders in thy Court."[23] When he summons his spirits to restore the Duke's natural appearance, Mago resembles Prospero summoning the spirits to perform a masque at the end of the operatic *Tempest*.

The style of the heroic play with its neat antitheses, its quick reversals, and its fantastic, whimsical conceptions of honor, is occasionally burlesqued in the discourse between the nobles. For example, in a passage for which there is no parallel in Cokain, Brunetto enters as an honorable enemy overcome in battle; he kneels to the Duke, who raises him but then asserts that he has been "charg'd . . . with a Crime will stain the Worth / You shew'd in Battel, and make Valour blush." The crime is loving the Duke's sister, who had been entrusted to her brother by their father with the command that she must not marry anyone of base blood. In the Duke's perverse view of things, Brunetto's love, therefore, makes the Duke "guilty":

[DUKE] . . . Now Sir, how far you have infring'd these Orders,
And brought a guilt unknown upon my head,
I leave yourself to judge: Confess your Crime,
And Torture shall revenge it; smother it,
And Torture shall extort it.

BRUNETTO. My charmed Soul
Came panting to my Lips to meet your Charge,
And beg forgiveness for its high presumption.
But since you talk of Tortures, I disdain
The servile Threats, and dare your utmost Rage;
I love the Princess, and have urg'd my passion,
Tho' I confess all hopeless of return.
This with a Soldiers freedom I avouch,
Who scorns to lodge that Thought he dares not own:
Now Sir, Inflict what punishment you please.
But let me warn you, that your vengeance reach
My head, or neither of us can have rest.

[DUKE]. Chains, Straw and Darkness! this is meer distraction!
To prison with him; you that waited on him
(*They lead off* BRUNETTO.)
Be now his Guard: Thin Diet and no Light;
Such usage may restore him—Vengeance thus
Converts to Charity. . . .[24]

The ridiculous alternative regarding torture, Brunetto's extravagant defiance, the letdown of the Duke's observation that this is all "distraction" and that Brunetto be imprisoned until he recovers—all burlesque the high ideals, exalted sentiments, and extreme behavior of the heroic play. "Chains, Straw and Darkness!" may be a mock-heroic expletive, or it may be merely a description of Brunetto's punishment (extremely modest in view of the "Torture" that had been threatened).

Although the characters are usually portrayed in the ironic manner of farce, they are occasionally seen with the insight of sympathetic comedy. As the Duke speaks to his counsellors, for example, he faces the problem of confusion in the world: is everyone else mad or is he? His response suggests that of Antipholus of Syracuse in Shakespeare's *Comedy of Errors:*

[DUKE]. The more I search, the more I am confounded,
Quite lost within a Labyrinth of wonders.
ALBERTO. Gods! how he speaks, as if all we were mad,
And he had done nothing.
[DUKE]. I will yet have patience:
Tell me my Lords, if you are very sure
That you are well and Masters of your Sense.
BARBERINO. If e're your Highness knew us so we are.
[DUKE]. Yet give me leave to think what I do know;
I can sustain no more. . . .[25]

The Duke strives to force himself and others to be realistic in his nightmare world.

A Duke and No Duke is a farce by any definition, but it includes enough of other kinds of comedy to make it more appealing than the ordinary farce. Scouten remarks on Tate's inconsistency in calling Brunetto the brother and the second son of the Duke of Savoy and on his failure to use some of the farcical material of his source. But the first seems a relatively trivial inconsistency, and Tate had enough for his purpose without using all that he could have from Cokain.[26] And his final product not only was appreciated by the monarch but by audiences well into the nineteenth century. *A Duke and No Duke* was made into a pantomime, a ballad opera, and a burletta; but it was most successful in the form Tate gave it, and the recorded performances of Tate's play greatly outnumber those of all the other versions. In this respect, its history is like that of *King Lear*: Tate's work was more successful than that of his "improvers." After 1746 Tate's farce was usually an afterpiece—a short, generally light work of one, two, or three acts that followed the main production—and at least once it was the afterpiece for his own *King Lear*.[27]

III Cuckolds-Haven

Tate's next play, *Cuckolds-Haven: or, An Alderman No Conjurer. A Farce,* was a redaction of *Eastward Ho!* by Jonson, Chapman, and Marston (Tate speaks of it simply as Jonson's) with some passages from the latter's *The Devil Is an Ass.* Tate, who thought well of his play, called it "no ill Imitation" of Jonson's work and blamed its failure on the fact that James Nokes, who had been a sensational success as Doodle in Ravenscroft's farce *The London Cuckolds,* was unable to play the role of Alderman Touchstone. As a consequence, Tate said, he had found it necessary to rewrite several scenes.[28]

But a more basic defect is the play's confusion of genre, of which Tate himself was aware; for, despite his calling the play a "farce" on the title page, he wondered in the dedication "if the Plot be not too regular for Farce, and ought not rather to have been call'd Comedy."[29] Tate's interest was in farcical action; but *Eastward Ho!* is a comedy of London life with a strongly realistic background; and *The Devil Is an Ass* is a satire in which, after a day on earth, the Devil decides that "Hell is A Grammar-school to this!"[30] The realistic background contrasts with the improbability of the farce, destroying the fun of the farce just as it lessens the interest of the realism. The accusation of Touchstone as witch (from *The Devil Is an Ass*) is too bitter for the careless laughter of farce, and the amoral and improbable ending leaves feelings that are aroused by the comedy and the satire unsatisfied.

Eastward Ho! is the story of the goldsmith Master Touchstone; his two apprentices, one industrious and the other prodigal; and his two daughters, one modest and the other proud. The prodigal apprentice, Quicksilver, is connected with another group of characters: his mistress Sindefy and an old usurer, Security, a jealous husband who keeps his young wife Winifred locked up. The proud daughter Gertrude is connected with still another group—her fiancé Sir Petronel Flash (he is after her money as she is after his title) and his friends. The industrious apprentice Golding and the modest daughter Mildred are attracted to each other. With the help of Quicksilver, Sir Petronel Flash tricks Gertrude out of her money and attempts to escape to Virginia with Winifred; but they are shipwrecked at Cuckolds-Haven, where they are captured.[31] Sir Petronel and Quicksilver repent in prison but are not forgiven by Alderman Touchstone until Golding has had himself arrested in order to soften the old man's heart. Winifred wins superiority over her repentant old husband Security; the latter gives Sindefy a dowry; Gertrude has learned her lesson; and all ends happily in a reasonably convincing manner.

The play contains several farcical scenes, principally in the portions attributed to Chapman, in which Quicksilver persuades the jealous old husband Security to assist in Sir Petronel's plan to elope with a lady (Quicksilver tells him she is the lawyer Bramble's wife, though actually she is Security's own wife Winifred): old Security then volunteers his wife's clothing for her disguise. Later, when both Security and Bramble meet Winifred masked but in her own clothes with Sir Petronel in a tavern, each of the husbands thinks she is the other's wife.

Tate reduces the play from five acts to three by cutting the dialogue substantially, but he adds some new farcical material, including a scene between Security and his servant Clogg based upon Pug's attempted seduction of Mrs. Fitzdottrel

(II, ii and iii) in *The Devil Is an Ass*. The conclusion is indebted to the same play, and it is here that the action seems inconsistent. Act III, Scene iv is at the Compter Prison, where Security meets Sir Petronel and Quicksilver. The three attempt to gain Touchstone's forgiveness by appearing repentant. When their scheme does not work, Security pretends to be possessed, while the other two accuse Touchstone of witchcraft and adultery. The lawyer Bramble takes one side and then the other, depending on which seems more likely to be profitable; and it appears that the fraud may succeed when it is revealed by accident as Security inadvertently uncovers the equipment by means of which he had seemed to foam at the mouth. Surprisingly, Touchstone is so much amused that he pardons everyone and even good-naturedly entreats his proud daughter to beg his pardon before all the characters adjourn to his house for a celebration. Nobody reforms; nobody repents; and Touchstone's forgiving everyone so easily violates both poetic justice and probability.

Norman Holland sees Tate's changes as suggesting "the authentic Restoration tone": the play reflects the view "that there is no morality commonly practiced by society by which these actions can be judged and . . . that in the face of this uncertainty, the best thing to do is relax, as Touchstone does, and get as much fun out of the doings as you can."[32] Certainly, it would hardly do in a Restoration comedy to have a merchant's values triumphant over those of the money-seeking aristocrat, the proud daughter who wants a title, and the overly restricted wife. And there is another reason for changing the ending: genuine repentance would seem a suddenly serious, even sentimental, breaking of the tone of the farce. There is much fun in *Cuckolds-Haven*—as Montague Summers has said, it probably had "considerable *brio* and verve" on the stage[33]—but it is not funny enough to make up for a thoroughly unsatisfactory conclusion.

IV The Island Princess

Even more popular on the Restoration stage than the plays of Shakespeare or Jonson were the dramas attributed to Beaumont and Fletcher. At least thirty-nine of these plays were performed during the Restoration;[34] and adaptations of thirteen were published. Most often adapted was Fletcher's *The Island Princess,* of which three alterations were made: the first anonymous, in 1669; the second by Tate in 1687; the third by Motteux in 1698.[35] Samuel Pepys, who saw the first redaction three times in four months early in 1669, remarked on the "good scene of a town on fire."[36]

Fletcher told a lively story uncomplicated by subplots. The King of Tidore has been imprisoned by the neighboring Governor of Ternata, and Tidore is ruled by his sister, the beautiful Quisara, who promises to marry the man who will free her brother. She assumes that her lover Ruy Dias will carry out the assignment, but the hero Armusia does so by distracting the King's captors with a fire in Ternata. The King wishes to give his sister's hand to Armusia, but the lady is reluctant. Ruy Dias urges his nephew Pyniero to assassinate the hero; and, when Quisara urges the same course of action, Pyniero pretends to undertake the assignment. Meanwhile, Armusia manages to gain entrance to Quisara's chamber to plead his case; there he confronts Ruy Dias, who arrives soon after. The next day the rivals fight a duel, which Armusia wins without killing his opponent.

By this time, Quisara has fallen in love with Armusia. However, the Governor of Ternata, disguised as a Moorish priest, has persuaded both the King and Quisara that Armusia must forswear his Christianity before he is allowed to marry the princess. Quisara attempts to convert her lover, but he refuses and is imprisoned. Armusia is about to be tortured—and Quisara in admiration of his steadfastness wishes to share his sufferings—when Ruy Dias arrives with rescuers. The Governor is exposed; and Armusia, reconciled with the King, is married to Quisara. Although the plot is single, the play achieves variety through its different kinds of action—the adventure of freeing the King in the first two acts, the love triangle in the middle portion of the play, and the religious-political conflict in the last act and a half.

The anonymous adapter of 1669 made two changes of importance. In his version, Quisara did not plot against Armusia's life; and her character was thereby preserved from blemish. And the scene of the fire (II, vi) was rewritten to add satiric remarks on the selfishness and dishonesty of carters who, during the fire, charged exorbitant rates for moving goods that were threatened and who also stole as much as they could. These remarks apparently alluded to Londoners' experience during the Great Fire of 1666[37] and, along with the spectacular staging, probably contributed to Pepys's appreciation of the scene. Tate used this 1669 version, changing some of the characters' names slightly (Ruy Dias is Ruidias; Soza, Sforza; Pyniero, Pymero), but not omitting any of Fletcher's fourteen important or named characters, although the role of Quisana, the princess's aunt, is reduced to a bit part, and she is not listed in the cast. By omitting short passages and several scenes, however, Tate reduces Fletcher's twenty-five hundred lines to about sixteen hundred.[38] Tate simplifies the action in Act I, and he omits Ruy Dias's plot to kill Armusia, thereby eliminating the plot against his life entirely.

The Princess's religious motives are purified by Tate. In Fletcher's play, Quisara was converted to Christianity by Armusia's noble behavior, and she did not make clear her conversion until Act V, where Armusia was about to be tortured. In Tate, however, she reveals in Act IV at the end of her attempt to convert Armusia that she already knows that Christianity is "heavenly all"[39] and that, in urging Armusia to change his religion, she has merely been testing his faith and, in his faith, him. The result is that Quisara is a Christian because of conviction rather than because of love and admiration of Armusia; she is a near-martyr for religion rather than for love. Perhaps Samuel Golden's suggestion that the adaptation was intended to reflect on the religious conflict of the day accounts in part for this change.[40] Feeling was especially strong in the spring of 1687, with James favoring, or appearing to favor, toleration: at the beginning of April he issued his first Declaration of Indulgence, and *The Island Princess* was performed at court on April 25.[41] In his Dedication, Tate says that the play shows "transcendent Vertue, Piety and Constancy successful,"[42] but it also "shows" the wisdom of toleration and the futility of punishing nonconformity. Yet the relationship of the adaptation to contemporary religious and political affairs is oblique; and Tate's *Island Princess* seems not to contain direct political allusions.

V Injur'd Love

John Webster enjoyed a modest popularity during the Restoration. Pepys thought *The White Devil* "a very poor play," but *The Duchess of Malfi* "a good play" on one occasion and "a sorry play" on another.[43] Both were occasionally revived. Tate's adaptation of *The White Devil* was apparently not acted, and he may not even have overseen its publication. The title page reads *Injur'd Love: Or, The Cruel Husband. A Tragedy. Design'd to be Acted at the Theatre Royal. Written by Mr. N. Tate, Author of the Tragedy call'd King Lear.* Unlike the rest of Tate's plays—indeed, unlike almost everything Tate published—the book appeared without either preface or dedication; and, though many title pages describe Tate as "Poet Laureate," no others refer to him as the "author" of the "tragedy" *King Lear*. Although *Injur'd Love* was neither performed nor republished, it was not forgotten. In 1731 Henry Fielding quoted from it several times in the notes of *The Tragedy of Tragedies;* but, on each occasion, he cited lines that had actually been written by Webster. For example, the opening lines of Webster's Act IV, "Untie your folded thoughts, and let them dangle loose as a bride's hair," are cited by Fielding as an example of "monstrous images in the tragic authors."[44]

Tate's adaptation was made between 1702 and 1707, at least fifteen years after he had stopped writing for the public theater.[45] Collier had objected to the immorality and profaneness of the stage; Tate had submitted his proposals for improving it; and sentimental comedy and domestic or pathetic tragedy with emphasis on romantic, filial, or marital faithfulness were in vogue. The pathetic tragedies of Otway, John Banks, and Southerne were favorites. As a result, Vittoria in *Injur'd Love* has ceased to be a "white devil" and is instead a faithful wife who resists the appeals of Brachiano:

> Beware my Lord! Orphans and Widows cries,

> Defrauded Labours starving Sighs are loud;
> But none, to draw down Vengeance from Above,
> No! None like the Complaints of injur'd Love.[46]

The accusations of Vittoria's mother Cornelia against her daughter are, then, false in Tate's version; and, more important, the heroine is wholly in the right in the trial scene. Hazelton Spencer objects that Vittoria's speeches in this scene "lose dramatic force because we know she is innocent" and that their "fierceness" is inconsistent with her earlier rejection of Brachiano.[47] They have a different kind of force in Tate's play, in which Vittoria is fiery, indignant, contemptuous of public opinion—but virtuous. At the same time, it is true that the scene lacks moral complexity; Tate is simplifying and making his characters black and white as he had done with others such as Richard II and Quisara. The women—Vittoria, Isabella, and Cornelia—stand virtuous, suffering undeservedly in the lustful, ambitious, cruel world of Brachiano and Flamineo.

For once Tate does not alter the ending significantly, but he combines scenes, tightens and clarifies the action, and clears up inconsistencies. For example, Tate does not bring Francisco to Padua with the conspirators, and thereby he removes the improbability of Francisco's being able to move around his brother-in-law's court unrecognized. It is at first surprising that the adapter who was interested in mad scenes in *King Lear* and in *The Ingratitude* should omit the scene in which Cornelia is mad; possibly this scene was considered a religious ceremony (a funeral) and was therefore objectionable on the reformed stage. The language is made more decorous, and the staging has also received some attention. The interview between Brachiano and Isabella (II, i) reminds one of the staging of *Brutus of Alba*: "A Grotto, Isabella leaning over a Fountain, Brachiano enters with a surly Deportment, she makes him a low Reverence, and moving forward a second or third time."[48] Some sixty lines later there is "A Noise under Ground," and twelve lines after that "Lightning and Thunder." The supernatural objections to unfaithfulness recall the similar objections in Tate's first play to the love of Brutus of Alba and the Queen of Syracuse.

VI *Tate's Adaptations*

From *King Lear* to *Injur'd Love* Tate's adaptations are intelligently made to fit new conditions and purposes. It has been conventional to scold the Restoration adapters—especially Tate—for ruining the plays, but only in *Eastward Ho!* and (from a political point of view) in *Richard II* did he actually choose to work with material unsuited to what he wanted to do. It is conventional also to look for the application of Neoclassic "rules" to the adaptations. Some tightening of the action, somewhat more decorum of character and language, and some increased respect for poetic justice are evident. On the other hand, comedy remains mixed with tragedy; the playwright does not seem to have gone much out of his way to achieve unity of place, time, or even action; and poetic justice, though it may operate in *King Lear,* has little effect on *Injur'd Love.*

Tate was interested in putting lively plays on the stage, and in the course of doing so he salvaged a large quantity of valuable material from what seemed to him period pieces. As he wrote in the Dedication to *The Island Princess,* "Those Defects in Manners, that were too palpable through the Work, must be imputed to the Age in which [Beaumont and Fletcher] Wrote; but still there are so many and transcending Beauties in all their Writings, that I judg'd it safest to Rob their Treasure. . . . The Metal is still the same. . . ."[49] The age was not interested in unpolished antiques or "Treasure," and the adaptations had to be given such conventional qualities of the new age as love stories, virtue in distress, scenes of lust, political relevance, and farcical action that would enable them to compete with contemporary dramas; or, it seemed, the plays themselves would die.

CHAPTER 7

Laureate Verse

LIKE MOST LAUREATE VERSE, Tate's odes, elegies, and other poems commemorating important public events and persons have little permanent value as poetry; but they are of interest for several other reasons. They are the panegyrical poetry of the laureate, or chief panegyrist, of the great age of panegyrical verse that followed the Revolution of 1688. As far as Tate himself is concerned, they exhibit once again the poet's ingenuity and his ability to achieve a measure of variety within the limits—for laureate verse, the narrow limits—prescribed by form and occasion. And these panegyrical poems are also interesting because of their connection with other arts: some of them attempt to imitate painting, and many show the effects of being written for music. A recent writer on John Blow has said that "only three new forms of English music were developed by the composers of the Restoration period: the elegy, the ode, and the opera, and it was Blow who instituted them all."[1] Tate contributed to these hybrid forms by writing the words, occasionally for Blow, but more often for Blow's great pupil, Henry Purcell.

The laureate poems should be read in their moral and social context. The emphasis on religion, morality, and decorum that extended from the realms of church and state into literature found expression in Jeremy Collier's demand for reform in the theater and in John Dennis's insistence that modern poetry was inferior to ancient poetry because modern writers did not recognize that poetry was essentially religious.[2] The laureates Shadwell and Tate were known as "honest" men, and Tate declared that it was the laureate's duty both to support religion and "to Celebrate the most exemplary Characters of the Age and Country in which he lives."[3] Such celebrations sometimes took the form of New Years' odes or songs praising the accomplishments of the past year and the promise of the new one; or birthday odes or songs, rejoicing in the character and accomplishments of the sovereign and the people's love for him; or elegies, celebrating the virtues and accomplishments of the deceased; or simply "Poems to . . . " or "Memorials of . . ." praising the same qualities in the living. The purposes of these writings were to present ideals as examples that others might be inspired to follow and to memorialize for future ages the great deeds and men of the poet's time—both of which are traditional aims of Classical and of Christian poetry.

The modern reader generally feels that these aims were conceived much too narrowly, and he finds such poems shallow in feeling, overconventional in design, and undiscriminating in their praise. But it should also be remembered that many of these verses were written to be sung to a musical accompaniment on a holiday or on a royal birthday to an audience of relatives, friends, and courtiers. The verses gave expression to the attitudes that were assumed to exist in the audience; and they succeeded, not by expressing fresh or original thoughts, but by saying in grand and simple terms what everybody was supposed always to have thought.

In these poems, the poet tended to state a thought abstractly and then hang images on it as illustration or embellishment; the results were pieces of decorative art, parts of court ceremonial. Such ceremonial poetry was certainly not new in Tate's age—it had flowered under Queen Elizabeth and had hardly declined under the Stuarts—but Amy Reed and A. H. Humphreys have suggested two reasons for its being especially prominent at the time Tate wrote. Miss Reed links some characteristics of this kind of poetry directly with the enthusiasm for moral reform:

> In the popular passion for the reform of manners and of literature, there was a distinct tendency to estimate a poem as excellent in proportion to the gravity of its subject, the morality of its sentiments, and the decorousness of its expression, ra-

> ther than to its originality of thought, its depth of feeling, or its rhythmic quality. If the poem, either by the wealth of its allusions or by its close imitation of the ideas of well-known classical literature, gave evidence of what in the popular mind was considered learning, it was even more highly valued.[4]

Humphreys writes of the "impoverished poetic sensibility" of the time, which, he suggests, may come from the traditional Classical education: "the demands for metrical excellence, allusive periphrasis, correctness, elegance, 'embellishments,' judgment, and 'easy and significant words' applied as it were from the outside are largely the responsibility of the classic creed."[5] Tate's laureate poems were written out of training of this sort, for readers who were trained to admire this kind of writing, and for occasions to which it was especially suited.

I *Elegies and Other Exemplary Characters*

In the Preface to his *Muse's Memorial of His Royal Highness, Prince George of Denmark,* Tate refers to his "Muse's Gallery of Honour, which She is furnishing with the Portraits of Illustrious Persons in Our Age and Nation."[6] The parallel between painting and poetry that the remark suggests is a traditional one going back at least as far as Aristotle, and it was the object of considerable attention during the seventeenth century. Dryden is said to have remarked on the similarity of the two arts twenty times or more,[7] and his *Parallel of Poetry and Painting* (1695) is an extended discussion of the subject. Dryden emphasized that the portrait painter, though he is less free to draw an ideal perfection than painters of other subjects, should sketch the better side of the face, "for an ingenious flattery is to be allowed to the professors of both arts [portrait painting and poetry], so long as the likeness is not destroyed."[8] After the realistic movements of the past two centuries, the modern reader will probably emphasize the qualifying clause more than Dryden intended. But Tate was thinking principally along the lines of the main clause when, in the Dedication to Prince George of *Portrait-Royal. A Poem upon Her Majesty's Picture Set up in*

Guild-Hall, he wrote of "Sculpture, Painting, and Poetry, whose Office it is to do just Honours to the Worthies of their Time, and transmit their Memories, for Glorious Examples, to Posterity."[9]

This poem expresses the sisterhood of the arts; it asserts the ability of poetry to paint; and it displays rather ostentatiously the poet's knowledge of Classical writers and modern painters. After a reluctant Muse has overcome her doubts and jealousy, she describes and praises the portrait of Queen Anne by John Closterman. Truth, Judgment, and Prudence are included in the artist's picture, but the Muse then describes other virtues for which "another Canvass" is needed—Charity, Constancy, Fortitude, and the like, as well as Eusebia (the Church of England) and Reformation. Each is "painted" by the Poet; for example,

> Let CONSTANCY, high-seated on a Rock,
> Dare Envy's Blast, and fickle Fortune's Shock.
> With chearful Aspect, such as can beguile
> The Rage of Storms, (and like Britannia's Isle)
> O'erlook the wrangling Waves, and at their Fury Smile[;]
> Her Standard fixt; and let this Motto flame
> On her spread Banner, EVERMORE THE SAME.[10]

After these figures have been described, the picture bursts into motion, and Painting is invited to use "all [her] Pencil's Force" to display England's recent victories on sea and land by Prince George and the Duke of Marlborough. The text is accompanied with superscript letters that refer the reader to about forty notes at the end of the poem, which explain references, cite Classical authorities on art, and refer to the example of modern painters.

The pictorial influence is also evident in the two elegies on queens, the most substantial of Tate's productions in this genre. The earlier of the two is *Mausolæum: A Funeral Poem On Our Late Gracious Sovereign Queen Mary;* as the title suggests, the setting is the mausoleum at Westminster Abbey:

> See where the Royal Shrine erected high,
> Threatning the Temple's Roof, as That the Sky;

With Starry Lamps and Banners blazing round,
And all the Pageantry of Death is crown'd.[11]

After Seraphs have decked the hearse with flowers, "four Matrons, deep in Sables clad" take their stations by the hearse, each taking a place in one of the "high-arch'd Inlets to the Sov'reign Hearse" (the poem was accompanied by an illustration of this scene.) The Matrons lament in turn: first Belgia, who sorrows for the death of a princess of the house of Orange; next Irene, the "Protestant Church of France," who laments her helplessness in exile and the death of the "Queen of Pity"; then Eusebia, who lists Queen Mary's virtues; and, finally, Britannia, who grieves for the death of the wise and gracious ruler. Then, at Eusebia's command, the roof of Westminster Abbey opens, showing "a Prospect to Eternal Day"; and Eusebia describes Mary's triumphant entry into Heaven, where she is greeted by "a Rev'rend Shade, his Head Mitred in Glory," who had been "Heav'ns Messenger to Us" and is now Mary's to Heaven—Archbishop Tillotson, whose death had preceded the Queen's by just over a month.

The posthumous *Poem Sacred to the Glorious Memory of her Late Majesty, Queen Anne* seems to be a series of pictures with commentary. First is a description of the Cave of Sorrow and of the "Loyal Muse's" arrival there to lament; at the invitation of the Queen of Sorrow, she describes the arrival of Britannia and Eusebia at court, with a picture of each:

August Britannia in that dismal Hour,
Half-blushing saw Her gen'rous Lion Cow'r;
He now lies grov'ling, whose once aweful Roar
Struck Terror to the Worlds remotest Shore:
Forlorn on Earth, Her Empire's Emblems lay;
Her Scepter dropt, as weary of its Sway,
Her Golden Globe, roll'd carelessly away;
Yet still an Air of Grandeur did confess,
Aweful in Tears, Majestick in Distress:[12]

Next, before giving the two mourners' laments, the Muse undertakes an elaborate forty-four-line metaphor describing the state of the court before and after the queen's death. The comparison is with a ship, a "First-Rate," pictured with flags flying and a gentle breeze, then storm-tossed, and finally wrecked; it attempts to convert into visual terms a state that was more felt than seen. Speeches by the two mourning ladies are followed by the Muse's own lament and by an appeal to the Duke of Buckingham to write a more worthy elegy.

Most of Tate's other elegies include the conventional pastoral settings, mourners' speeches, decking of the hearse, and arrival of the deceased person in heaven; and almost all are written in heroic couplets. But each also has distinctive qualities, for Tate seems to have made a point of adjusting the form to the particular subject. Thus, the elegy for John Playford (1687) was written to be set to music, provided by Henry Purcell. Excluding "repeats," it is about thirty lines long; and it is a précis of the seventeenth-century pastoral elegy. Shepherds are urged to lament for "Pious Theron"; Nature ("Rending Mountains, weeping Fountains, groaning Dales, and ecchoing Vales") will teach them how. If Innocence, Piety, or Art could have saved him, "belov'd of Pan, and dear to Phebus Train," they would have. The Muses are then asked to bring roses and to strew the hearse; and when the roses wither, the Muses are to "crown it with a lasting verse." However, roses, verse, and tomb will all decay: only Theron's name will live, smelling even sweeter than the roses. The Chorus then asserts that there is no need to lament, for the dead man was prepared by Harmony and Love to join the immortal Choir "at first approach."[13]

In the elegy on Charles II, on the other hand, in spite of suggestions of the pastoral (for example, Charles passes on "his Flock, / To the next Shepherd of the Royal Stock"), Tate emphasizes the disorder resulting from Charles's death and the reestablishment of order in James—the point of view of *The Second Part of Absalom and Achitophel.*[14] The elegy on Ormond and Ossory, entitled *Carmen Pastorale-Nauticum,* is a dialogue between the shepherd Thirsis and the sailor Damon lamenting the deaths of the great Irish soldier, statesman, and patron of poets, and his son, who had achieved the rank of admiral before his death in 1680.[15]

However, the shepherds are dismissed at the beginning of

the elegy on the Countess of Dorset (1691), the wife of Tate's patron and one of Queen Mary's favorite ladies-in-waiting. Nature laments, but the skies rejoice at regaining one of their stars. At the urn stand the Graces, Youth, Beauty, Innocence, Zeal, Piety, Prayer, "Belief and Hope transfigur'd to Despair," Charity, Compassion, and Death; the last, though he triumphs over the living, who must do without the Lady, cannot be victorious over the Lady herself—for she is in Heaven.[16] The elegy for Archbishop Tillotson (1695), on the other hand, is full of biblical metaphors. The Archbishop's death is like Samuel's; his tomb is to be decorated with Syrian lilies and Sharon roses, and the perfume will be "Arabia's Spice" and "Gilead's Balm." The speaker of the elegy will be like the voice from Elijah's tomb. Eusebia, the Church of England, laments the death of her "ruling Pastor," whose "Crook . . . bloom'd like Aaron's Wand." "Britain's State" laments him as the conqueror of Atheism and of Rome; his "Temper [is] calm, and Sanatively cool, / As Jordan's Current, or Bethesda's Pool."[17]

Another elegy is a "Consolatory Poem" (1698) addressed to John, Baron Cutts (1661-1707), on the death in childbirth of his eighteen-year-old second wife. Cutts was the distinguished soldier, poet, and friend of poets who is best known in literary history for helping Richard Steele obtain his commission and for receiving the dedication of Steele's *Christian Hero* (1701). "In a lonsome Vale" Lysander grieves, ignoring "the glitt'ring Furniture of War" lying unused about him. Mars, Minerva, Apollo, the Muses, the Graces, the Virtues, Britannia, Peace, and Conquest descend from the hills to address him. Mars urges him to live "for Glory's sake"; Minerva praises the dead lady; and Apollo, who wishes to comfort him or at least to share his grief, sings a short funeral poem describing the procession at Laurinda's funeral and the Lady's arrival in Heaven. Finally, Britannia mentions William's name, and Lysander returns to duty. The poem is pictorial and is said to have inspired an allegorical print by Thomas Wall.[18]

Three elegies are for men of the law. The brief poem on Joseph Washington (1694), "Late of the Middle Temple" and a contributor with Tate and Dryden to the translation of

Lucian that was finally published in 1711, laments the death of a man of unusual ability, virtue, and learning.[19] Tate concludes with a comparison of Washington with Marvell and Milton:

> Scarcely in Marvel's keen Remarks we find
> Such Energy of Wit and Reason join'd.
> Great Milton's Shade with pleasure oft look'd down,
> A Genius to applaud so like his Own.[20]

The elegy for the Justice of the Peace Ralph Marshall (1700) is notable for Tate's statement in his address "To the Reader" that he has tried "to Write his Elegy in the same honest Plainess and Sincerity with which [Marshall] Liv'd. I confess I was more concern'd for Resemblance, in this Piece, than for Fineness of Strokes or Embellishment of Colours." The style, then, is deliberately not polished, as in the following:

> To Books no Stranger; Books that were of Use
> He read, and into Practice did reduce:
> Studied to know what Sages understood;
> Yet less he studi'd to be Skill'd than Good.[21]

In the elegy (1702) on Sir George Treby (1644?-1700), who had been solicitor general, attorney general, and chief justice of common pleas, Tate's admiration seems not to have been ill-placed; for John Evelyn wrote that Treby "was a learned man in his profession, of which we have now few, never fewer.[22] Tate had published a sixty-five-line "character" of Treby in 1699, which he included with the elegy in 1702.[23] The latter is in dialogue form: it includes the inevitable procession of allegorical mourners at the tomb—Charity, Compassion, Patience, and so on—and laments that there is no one worthy of succeeding the Justice.

II The Muse's Bower

Near the end of his career, Tate wrote a public poem modeled upon Spenser's *Prothalamion* and imitative of the Elizabethan poet's style in imagery, diction, and sound effects:

The Muse's Bower, An Epithalamium (1713), which celebrates the marriage of the Earl of Oxford's daughter, Lady Elizabeth Harley, to the Marquis of Caermarthen. It precedes the period of Spenserian imitation by more than two decades, but it seems to have been overlooked by scholars who have studied Spenser's influence in the eighteenth century.

The poet invokes Love's Queen (not the Cyprian Goddess, but "Hymen's Daughter and Diana's Friend"), who sponsors Albion lands "where Thames the Medway weds" and who "make[s] the Verdure of the Vale revive":

> Forthwith he saw a glorious Grove ascend,
> Whose burden'd Boughs with Golden Apples bend,
> Fairer than in Alcinous Orchard grew,
> And Bow'rs Adonis Garden never knew,
> Nor Spencer's richer Fancy ever drew.
> Spencer, who Art and Nature could command,
> And great Eliza charm'd to Faery Land.[24]

He praises "Anna" and paints her sleeping on a flowery bank surrounded with Graces and Cupids, whose activities are described in terms that suggest Pope's sylphs in the revised version of *The Rape of the Lock,* which was published less than a year later.[25] To a modern reader, the eighteenth-century poetic diction seems out of keeping with the Spenserian character of the poem as a whole:

> Some Wantons leap into the Lake, to try
> If there, for Oars, their Pinions they could ply;
> Pleas'd that their Plumes a purple Lustre dart,
> That made the frighted Fountain-Nymphs to start.[26]

Fame awakens Anna and tells of Neptune's praise of London, England's victory over the Dragon of Rome through the marriage of William and Mary, and the bridegroom's "victories" (*The Dictionary of National Biography* describes a checkered naval career);[27] the marriage is blessed, and the bride herself is praised:

> Hymen, who lent till now a gracious Ear,
> The solemn Signal gave for Silence Here:

Pleas'd but Constraind to intercept their Song,
Because it made his Guests attend too long.[28]

The last two lines suggest the refrain of Spenser's poem: "Against the brydale day, which is not long: / Sweete Themmes, runne softly, till I end my song." Tate had also echoed them a few lines earlier, when he wrote: "Whilst Hymen, hearkning for the Bridal Song, / Complains, we make his Tryumph wait too long."[29] Although *The Muse's Bower* is in heroic couplets and does not include the procession down the river of the *Prothalamion,* the setting is similar; and the pictorial style, leisurely pace, frequent alliteration, and Spenserian diction result in a fairly successful effort to imitate the Elizabethan manner.

III *Odes and Songs*

The laureate ode, usually celebrating a royal birthday or the New Year, has a very low critical reputation, stemming mainly from the much-ridiculed productions of Colley Cibber. According to Broadus, it was not until the brief tenure of Nicholas Rowe (1715-18) that odes for New Years and birthdays "became the Laureate's recognized duty."[30] But much responsibility for establishing the tradition may be assigned to Tate, who published seven birthday odes (two in 1693 and one each in 1694, 1697, 1707, 1711, and 1715) and eight New Years' odes (1693, 1698, 1702, 1703 1705, 1706, 1707, and 1708). Since he is known to have written one other birthday ode (1699) that was apparently not published,[31] it seems likely that there were still more that did not see print. Tate appears to have used the terms "ode" and "song" interchangeably in referring to these poems: all were written to be set to music and "performed," and they have the same obvious themes—joy for the occasion, praise of the sovereign's victories (William) or virtues as a loving ruler (Mary or Anne), the country's good luck in having such a ruler, and the expectation of an even more glorious future.

By the time Tate wrote his laureate odes, he had acquired considerable experience in writing for music: he had collaborated with Purcell in *Dido and Aeneas;* he had written the Ode for Saint Cecilia's Day in 1685, two years before Dryden's first ode for this celebration; and his major undertaking of the early 1690's was the metrical version of the Psalms. Writing for music, of course, imposed certain restrictions. When Motteux published Tate's Dublin Ode in *The Gentleman's Journal,* he observed that the poet had "given Mr. Purcell an opportunity, by the easiness of the words, to set them to Music with his usual success."[32] In 1698, when Tate published his odes on the king's birthday and on New Years, he too complained tactfully about the limitations imposed upon him by the music: "The Glorious Occasion upon which these Odes were written . . . requir'd the utmost Liberties of Poetry; but I was Confin'd (for the Present) to such Measures and Compass as the Musical Performance would admit; upon which Consideration the Reader's favourable allowance is requested. . . ."[33]

Something of the technique of writing for music in Tate's time may be seen by applying to the laureate's first birthday ode (1693) the ten criteria for musical odes derived by Robert M. Myers from Neoclassic critics: that the ode be an excellent poem, historical or narrative in form, using sentiments rather than images, written in the lyric style, impassioned, varied in its passions, simple, adaptable to a musical setting, and flexible for reversal of lines and repetition.[34] The words for the ode were published in the April, 1693, issue of *The Gentleman's Journal.* Part of Purcell's music was included separately in the same issue of the periodical, and it became one of the most often anthologized of the composer's works.[35]

Hark, hark—
The Muses and the Graces call
To celebrate this Festival:
Britain now thy Cares beguile,
Bless the Day that blest our Isle:
'Tis Sacred—Bid the Trumpet cease,
And War devote this Day to Peace.

Crown the Altar, deck the Shrine;
Behold the bright Seraphick Throng

Prepar'd our Harmony to join;
The Sacred Quire attend too long;
Crown the Altar deck the Shrine.

Expected Spring at last is come
Attir'd in all her Youthful Bloom.
She's come, and pleads for her delay,
She waited for Maria's Day.
She waited for Maria's Day,
Nor would, before that Morn, be Gay.

April, who till now has mourn'd,
Claps for Joy his Sable Wing,
To see within his Orb return'd
The choicest Blessings he could bring,
Maria's Birth-Day and the Spring.

Departing, thus you'll hear him say,
Crown'd with the Honour of this Day,
I envy not the Pride of May.
On Flora's Charms let her enlarge;
A Saint and Beauty was my Charge.

Happy, happy, past expressing
Britain, if thou know'st thy Blessing:
Home bred Faction ne're Alarm Thee,
Other Mischief cannot harm Thee.

Happy Realm, beyond expressing,
Such a Royal Pair possessing;
Caesar bears thy Toils of War,
Maria thy Domestick Care;
Their's the Trouble, Thine the Blessing:
Happy, happy, past expressing.

While for a Righteous Cause He Arms,
  The wondrous Hero scapes
  From Death in thousand Shapes,
Still safe, still foremost in Alarms.

Let guilty Monarchs shun the Field,
The active Part to Others yield;

In Person Triumph, but by Proxy Fight;
The pious Prince alone can Dangers slight.

Return, return—The Thought of War
On this Auspicious Day forbear,
When Britain only should her Joy proclaim;
And to Disarm approaching Harm,
Repeat Maria's Name.

CHORUS.

Kindly treat the Genial Day,
And your Homage 'twill repay,
Bequeathing Blessings on our Isle,
The tedious Minutes to beguile;
Till Conquest to Maria's Arms restore
Peace and her Hero, to depart no more.[36]

Particularly noticeable is the poem's flexibility for music in providing lines that may be reversed ("Repeat Maria's Name" or "Maria's Name Repeat") and that will endure repitition without absurdity. The last lines of most of the stanzas are well suited to this kind of treatment. Similarly, the imperative lines in the early part of the poem may be hurled back and forth between singers—an opportunity of which Purcell took full advantage with "Britain now thy Cares Beguile."

Other Neoclassical criteria include metrical precision, simplicity, and provision for a chorus: these, too, Tate's ode has. It allows some opportunity for the composer in variety of mood, though there is a lack of contrast: the summoning of the first stanza changes to the joyous expectation of the second, the delight of the third, the awakening from darkness of the fourth, the triumph of the fifth through seventh, the martial mood of the eighth and ninth, and the joy of the tenth. The style is lyric, moderately polished; and the poem states—and to a modest degree creates—passion. The writer of an ode for music is supposed to prefer sentiments to images, partly to avoid giving the musician an allegedly irresistible temptation to "imitate" or "paint the passions"; but Tate has Spring welcomed at the altar, and April of the "Sable Wing" departs.

The narrative pattern that an ode is expected to follow is very slight here, as it is also in Tate's other odes for music.

The final requirement—which Myers and the Neoclassic critics put first—is the point at which Tate's ode and most official odes of other poets are found wanting: literary quality. Although the critics seem to have felt literary excellence was necessary to inspire the musician,[37] Purcell's music seems not to have suffered here. In spite of this deficiency, however, the laureate odes are not as artless (in the poorer sense) as they may seem to be. Undoubtedly, too, this habit of writing verse to be sung affected Tate's style in other poems, encouraging him to keep the moods themselves simple and to express thoughts very clearly in lines that could be easily followed.

Two of Tate's odes (though they lack the name in the title) are more explicitly literary in their inspiration. One is *Britannia's Prayer for the Queen* (1706), which is a paraphrase of one of Lewis Maidwell's Latin poems. The beginning is effective:

> How justly now might I aspire
> To Mighty Pindar's Force and Fire,
> When Gods and God-like Kings He did rehearse,
> And Crown'd Them with Immortal Verse
> Worth all their Statues, by the skilfull'st Hand,
> That only could for short-lived Ages stand.
> But the Possession of the Golden Lyre,
> Where All the Charms of Harmony Conspire,
> The Muse to Pindar did confine:
>   Pindar Alone she does permit
>   In Wits sublimest Orb to sit,
> And, like the Sun, without a Rival shine.[38]

The ideas of the greatness of the occasion and the poet's inadequacy are given forceful and graceful expression. In the previous year Tate had expressed similar ideas in his *Triumph, or Warriours Welcome,* in which he apologized that his strength was ". . . now Reduc'd, by Injuries and Age, / Below the bold Efforts of Epic Rage; . . ." He needs the "Genius of proportion'd Rage" to sing:

Maro's too Modest, Homer's Heat too Cold,
Her Raving Pindar's self scarce so sublimely bold.
From Faery-Land let Britain's Spencer Rise,
And Milton soar his loftier Paradise,
Still Martial Merit mounts into Superiour Skies.[39]

This poem begins with an imitation of the Prologue to Shakespeare's *Henry V* ("O for a Muse of Fire"): "O for a Muse of Flame, the Daring Fire / That Blenheim's Battling Warriours did inspire. . . ." The imitation of *Henry V* is not inappropriate, of course; for allusion to Agincourt is natural enough in a poem celebrating Blenheim. But the poem is not as well sustained and is much thinner than Addison's poem on the same subject.

In form, Tate's odes and odelike poems are English Pindarics, descended from those of Cowley and Flatman. To English poets of the day, there does not seem to have been a sharp distinction between an ode and a hymn: Addison published his "Spacious Firmament on High" as an "Ode" in *Spectator* 465 (August 23, 1712) only four days after Steele had published a translation of Psalm 114, which he called "an admirable Ode" in *Spectator* 461. According to George N. Shuster, there were four "great exemplars" of the ode for English writers—Pindar, Horace, Anacreon, and David the psalmist.[40] To David, Tate devoted more attention in the 1690's than he spent on his laureate poems.

CHAPTER 8

The Psalms

UNTIL THE EIGHTEENTH century the Lutheran tradition of originality in composing hymns had little effect on church song in England; instead of freely composed hymns, metrical versions of the Psalms were sung during the services of both Anglicans and Puritans. Although translations had been made for this purpose earlier, it was at the beginning of Elizabeth's reign, when the Marian exiles brought back to England the Calvinistic tradition of singing metrical versions of the Psalms to a limited number of established tunes, that the need for a satisfactory metrical version produced a Psalter that was generally accepted. In 1562 John Day published *The Whole Booke of Psalmes,* often called "Sternhold and Hopkins" after the two principal contributors, and later known as the "Old Version." The British Museum has copies of over six hundred editions of it published between 1562 and 1828.[1]

The list of English poets who translated some or all of the Psalms in meter includes Sir Thomas Wyatt, the Earl of Surrey, Sir Philip Sidney, Spenser, George Herbert, Richard Crashaw, Henry Vaughan, and Milton, as well as many lesser men; by 1695 there were more than one hundred complete or partial translations.[2] As Hallett Smith has remarked, the practice of writing metrical versions of the Psalms had an important influence on the development of English verse during the sixteenth century, especially on metrics.[3] Although some of these versions were not seriously intended for use in churches, many were; George Wither's translation—for which the poet wrote a lengthy *Preparation to the Psalter* (1619)—was intended for church use and received the support of James I. And the king himself translated some of the Psalms, although the versions published as his were almost entirely by other writers.[4]

One reason for the continuing flow of Psalters was dissatisfaction with the Old Version of 1562. Despite some revision, the old translation seemed archaic, inelegant, and harsh to sophisticated seventeenth-century ears. William Whittingham, for example, had rendered the third verse of Psalm 23 in lines that were awkward verbally (the second line) and metrically (the third and fourth lines):

> And when I feel my self near lost,
>   then doth he me home take,
> Conducting me in his right paths
>   even for his own Name's sake.[5]

For Dryden, Sternhold and Hopkins represented clumsiness of verse and stupidity: in the Preface to *All for Love*, "a legitimate son of Sternhold" was an epithet applied to the well-to-do person who does not realize that he writes bad poetry;[6] Tom Sternhold and Tom Shadwell were bracketed together in the last line of *Religio Laici*; and Dryden's portraits of Shadwell and Settle in *The Second Part of Absalom and Achitophel* were preceded by an allusion to those "Poor slaves in meter, dull and addle-pated, / Who rhyme below ev'n David's psalms translated" (11. 402-3).

Something of what the age wanted can be seen by comparing Sternhold's simple translation of the first two verses of Psalm 34 (which are far from his worst) with the more sophisticated translation by Tate and Brady. In Tate's day, Sternhold's version read:

> I will give laud and honour both
>   unto the Lord always,
> Also my mouth for evermore
>   shall speak unto his praise.
> I do delight to laud the Lord
>   in soul, in heart, and voyce:
> That humble men and mortifi'd:
>   may hear and so rejoyce.

Earlier, "Also" in the third line had been "And eke," and the sixth line had been "in soul and eke in voyce." Tate and Brady wrote:

> Thro' all the changing Scenes of Life,
> in trouble, and in Joy,
> The Praises of my God shall still
> my Heart and Tongue employ.
> Of his Deliv'rance I will boast,
> till all that are distrest
> From my Example Comfort take,
> and charm their Griefs to rest.[7]

To a taste that admired the latter version, the former seemed old-fashioned and drab.

I *The* New Version

Tate and Nicholas Brady (1659-1726) were excellently qualified to respond to the demand for a new version. Tate, the son of a verse-writing Puritan minister, had some experience in writing for music; he enjoyed the favor of King William and the pious Queen Mary; and he had the prestige of the laureateship and was fond of emphasizing the laureate's duty to "the Temple." His collaborator's qualifications were equally good: Brady was a fashionable clergyman who had held various livings in Ireland and in England and had served as chaplain to William, Mary, and Princess Anne; he also had literary pretensions and had written a tragedy and a successful "Ode for St. Cecilia's Day" (1692). Like Tate, he was one of Dorset's protégés: he had dedicated his play to his patron in 1692 and ten years later was appointed by him to the rectory at Straford-upon-Avon.[8]

As for the division of labor between the collaborators, H. L. Bennett suggests that we "attribute the ornate work, in which some have even suggested an occasional aid from his patron Dryden, to Tate," or that "Brady [was] the theological, Tate the poetical workman throughout."[9] That Tate was the "poetical workman" seems much the more likely; for Tate was the senior partner, the man with fewer other duties, and the more experienced poet. He probably did most of the versifying while Brady concerned himself principally with matters of accuracy and doctrine.

Aware that there would be opposition to a new version, the authors were exceedingly cautious in presenting their translation. Psalms 1-5 were published first, probably in 1694; next Psalms 1-8 appeared; then the Archbishop of Canterbury, Tillotson, gave his imprimatur to the first twenty on November 7, 1694; and they were published early the next year. There was even another edition of 1695 with seventy Psalms, before the full one hundred and fifty appeared late in 1696 with a dedication to King William.[10] Revisions were made at each stage. On December 3, the King in Council declared that since Tate and Brady "with their utmost Care and Industry" had completed their *New Version*, it be "Allowed and Permitted to be used in all such Churches, Chapels, and Congregations, as shall think fit to receive the same." The Bishop of London added his recommendation two years later.[11]

However, Tate and Brady were not satisfied: by 1698 they had completed an extensive revision, which appeared in that year, and then was followed by still another revision. Editions stemming from both of these 1698 versions were published for the next century; only after 1800 did the text given in the 1698 edition printed by Hodgkin become standard.[12] Hodgkin's edition advertised "A Supplement to the New Version," a work that seems not to have been printed until 1700, but thereafter was expanded through several editions.[13] The *Supplement* contains "An Introduction to all Lovers of Psalmody," with instructions on the music; a large number of tunes; alternative versions of some of the Psalms; translations of the Canticles, the Creed, the Lord's Prayer, and the Commandments; several hymns, including the well-known "While Shepherds watch'd their Flocks by Night"; and tables fitting the Psalms to the tunes. Queen Anne approved the *New Version* and the *Supplement* on July 30, 1703.[14] As we have seen, Tate received some financial support for his work on the Psalms from both William and Anne.

Although there was said to be opposition from booksellers who had large stocks of the Old Version,[15] as well as from conservative clergymen and laymen, the *New Version* replaced the old one fairly rapidly in many parishes in and around London, and also in some of the less rural parishes elsewhere. Like the Old Version, it was frequently bound with the Bible or the Prayer Book and was not replaced in general use until well into the nineteenth century. In America, where the first edition of Tate and Brady was published in New York in 1710, it had made some headway before Tate's death.[16]

Of the translations of the Psalms that are included as hymns in modern hymnals, one ("All people that on earth do dwell," from a rendering of Psalm 100 published in 1561) is associated with the Old Version, and several are from the *New*: "Thro' all the changing scenes of Life" (Psalm 34); "As pants the Hart for cooling streams" (Psalm 62); "Have mercy, Lord, on me" (Psalm 51); "O God of Hosts, the mighty Lord" (Psalm 84); "With Glory clad, with Strength array'd" (Psalm 93); "O 'twas a joyful sound to hear" (Psalm 122); "My Soul with patience waits" (beginning with line 9 of Psalm 130); and "O Praise ye the Lord, prepare your glad voice" (Psalm 139).

There were several influences on the *New Version*. One consisted of the previous versions which the translators consulted and from which they borrowed. Another was the obligation to traditional tunes and measures: if a new translation was to succeed in the churches, it had to be written to fit well-known tunes. And—most compelling in the demands for a *new* version—the translation must have style, which, for the age and the "Quality and Gentry" for whom the translation was especially designed, meant polish and elegance of diction and imagery and smoothness of sound and meter. Still another influence was contemporary history, whose effect appears in the allusions to the Popish Plot and the Revolution of 1688.

Some borrowings by the authors of the *New Version* from Miles Smyth's translation (1668) have been pointed out,[17] and no doubt they borrowed from many others. Of particular interest to students of literature is the relation of Psalms 80-88 in the *New Version* to Milton's translation of them in common measure. The debt is slight; but, unless Milton and Tate had a common source, it seems definite: both poets begin

Psalm 82 with identical lines, "God in the great assembly stands," and Milton begins Psalm 86: "Thy *gracious* ear, O Lord, encline, / O hear me *I thee pray*." The italics were supplied by Milton in the 1673 edition of his poems to indicate words that were not in the Hebrew text; Tate and Brady's second line repeats Milton's first (including the word "gracious") with the necessary adjustment in meter: "To my Complaint, O Lord my God, / thy gracious Ear incline."

Tate and Brady began by being subservient to existing tunes, but they ultimately encouraged the addition of more tunes and more variety in church music for singing. Beginning even with the trial edition of twenty Psalms published in 1695, the translators were careful to emphasize on the title page that their Psalms were "fitted to the Tunes used in Churches." Most of these tunes were in "common measure" or "double common measure," which consists of stanzas of four or eight lines with alternating lines of eight and six syllables, also described as 8.6.8.6. Most of the translations in Sternhold and Hopkins were in this pattern. Ninety-four of the Tate-Brady Psalms are in common measure, with rhyme patterns of *abab* or *abcb*; in 1696 they were printed in four-line stanzas, but thereafter in eight-line stanzas (*ababcdcd*). The reader is informed that the common-measure Psalms "may be sung to any of the most usual Tunes; namely, York-tune, Windsor-tune, St. David's, Litchfield, Canterbury, Martyrs, St. Mary's, alias Hackney, St. Anne's Tune, &c.," which he could locate in the popular collections of hymn tunes.[18] Thirty-six of the Psalms in the *New Version* are in long measure (8.8.8.8.), printed in six-line or in eight-line stanzas. Six are in short measure (6.6.8.6.), although in 1696 two of them had been in common measure: the revisions of 1698 had extended even to changing the metrical form.

The other three Psalms (136, 148, and 149) have different patterns ("peculiar measure"), but each is fitted to an existing tune. However, the twenty-six alternative translations in the *Supplement* were in peculiar measure, and the result was that still more hymn tunes were needed for them. So it came about that, though it was very conservative in the tunes it called for originally, the *New Version* still came "to mark the beginning of a new advance in the music of the English

Church" and to stimulate the considerable discussion of church music that took place during the early years of the eighteenth century.[19]

The effects of the elegant diction that Tate and Brady employed may be seen both at their best and at their worst in Psalm 24. The opening lines have much of the strength of the Prayer Book version:

> This spacious Earth is all the Lord's,
> the Lord's her fulness is;
> The World, and they that dwell therein,
> by sov'reign right are his.
> He fram'd and fix'd it on the Seas,
> and his Almighty Hand
> Upon inconstant Floods has made
> the stable Fabrick stand.

The first lines give a sense of spaciousness; and the last four, with the stress of alliteration on the verbs "fram'd and fix'd" and the strong rhymes "made" and "stand," convey a sense of strength. "And they that dwell therein," a restoration of "biblical" language from the Prayer Book or the Authorized Version, was "and its Inhabitants" in 1696. Here the translators seem to have recognized the limits of elegant wording, at least in their second thoughts. Hopkins had rendered these lines rather inelegantly in the Old Version:

> The earth is all the Lord's, with all
> her store and furniture:
> Yea his is all the world and all
> that therein doth endure.
> For he hath fastly founded it
> above the seas to stand
> And plac'd below [earlier: laid alow] the liquid floods,
> to flow beneath the land.

Yet the last verses of the Psalm in the *New Version* miss the triumph of the Prayer Book version: "Lift up your heads, O ye gates, and be ye lift up, ye everlasting doors: and the King of glory shall come in. Who is the King of glory: even the

Lord of hosts, he is the King of glory."[20] Tate and Brady wallow in such elegant diction as "Erect," "unfold," "entertain," and "shining Train"; for triumph has been confused with glitter:

> Erect your Heads, ye Gates unfold,
> in state to entertain
> The King of Glory: see he comes
> with all his shining Train.
> Who is the King of Glory? who?
> The Lord of Hosts renown'd:
> Of Glory he alone is King,
> who is with Glory crown'd.

Some of the Psalms reflect the political experience of Tate, the Tory disdainful of plots and the Whig opponent of King James and the supporter of William. For example, Psalm 18, v. 43, which the Prayer Book renders as "Thou shalt deliver me from the strivings of the people: and thou shalt make me the head of the heathen," becomes a defense of divine right by the author of *The Second Part of Absalom and Achitophel:*

> Our factious Tribes, at strife till now,
> by God's appointment me obey;
> The Heathen to my Scepter bow,
> and foreign Nations own my Sway.

Even more explicit is the translation of Psalm 37, vv. 12-13, which the Prayer Book version renders as "The ungodly seeketh counsel against the just: and gnasheth upon him with his teeth. The Lord shall laugh him to scorn: for he hath seen, that his day is coming." Tate has

> While sinful Crowds with false Design,
> Against the righteous Few combine,
> And gnash their Teeth, and threatning stand.
> God shall their empty Plots deride,
> And laugh at their defeated Pride:
> He sees their Ruin near at hand.

Finally, in Psalm 108, vv. 40-41, Tate and Brady justify the Revolution of 1688:

> The Prince who slights what God commands
> Expos'd to scorn, must quit his Throne;
> And over wild and desart Lands,
> Where no path offers, stray alone:
> Whilst God, from all afflicting Cares,
> Sets up the humble Man on high;
> And makes in time his num'rous Heirs
> With his encreasing flocks to vie.

Here the Prayer Book has "Though he suffer them to be evil intreated through tyrants: and let them wander out of the way in the wilderness; Yet helpeth he the poor out of misery: and maketh him housholds like a flock of sheep."

II *The Defense of the* New Version

Despite care and tact in introducing the *New Version*, Tate and Brady soon found their work the subject of controversy. Many congregations rejected it, including that of Saint Catherine Cree, which had been Brady's until he resigned it in 1696. On November 22, 1697, Brady preached the Saint Cecilia's Day sermon at Saint Bride's church on the text of 2 Chron. 5: 13-14, which he published under the title of *Church-Musick Vindicated*. Although he was interested in the broad subject of church music, he referred to the Psalms several times and might have had in mind the opponents of the *New Version* when he asserted that "Religion, however mistaken or misrepresented by some, is the most entertaining thing in Nature . . . And therefore nothing has done her a greater prejudice . . . than the false Draughts made of her by some sort of People, who would have her consist in Moroseness and Austerity" and have therefore made her "Handmaid" Music "run the hazard of being Discarded from her Service."[21]

The controversy over the *New Version* itself reached a climax in 1710, when the executors of the estate of Dr. William Beveridge (1637-1708), Bishop of Saint Asaph, published the bishop's one-hundred-and-twenty-page earnest and good-tempered but firm attack upon the *New Version,* entitled *A Defence of the Book of Psalms* [i.e., the Old Version] . . . *With Critical Observations on the late New Version, Compar'd with the Old.* After more than four pages devoted to listing his previous writings, the bishop, who seems to have been erudite and conscientious but "not in advance of his age,"[22] begins his attack on the *New Version.* Partly, his arguments are the traditional objections of conservatism anywhere: the version is indeed "new," and the "new in Religion, at the best, is unnecessary"; it is "light and airy" whereas the Old Version is "grave and solid"; and the elegant style of the *New Version* will expire with the age in which it is written.[23] He is also disturbed by its inaccuracy as a translation; simple people, he argues, will take it for Scripture and will be seriously misled. As examples, he quotes two verses (Psalm 37, vv. 34 and 91) which might seem to imply that the psalmist approved of the theater, an idea that would be unacceptable to some of the more Puritanical users of the book:

> With longing Eyes thou soon shalt see
> The Wicked's fatal Tragedy,
> And as a glad Spectator sit.
>
> Thou only shalt look on, and see
> The Wicked's deserv'd Tragedy,
> And count the Sinner's mournful Gains.[24]

The comparison between the sufferings of the damned and a tragedy (or a comedy) is a traditional one, suggested by Tertullian in *De Spectaculis* (ca. 200 A.D.).[25] However, the bishop is concerned with its practical effect on ignorant readers; and he imagines at some length a man's justifying his attendance at the theater on the basis of these passages. They are, he insists, inaccurate as an expression of the "Inspiration of God."[26] His objection (and Tate's reply, discussed below) brings into focus the different points of view of the practical churchman, who fears that the ignorant will misunderstand, and the poet, who is concerned with his art and has little sympathy for an unsophisticated audience.

It was in 1710 also that Tate's thirty-eight-page answer to the opponents of the *New Version* appeared. Entitled *An Essay for Promoting of Psalmody,* it had no author's name on the title page, but Tate signed the dedication to Queen Anne. The argument of the first two chapters is that the Psalms are useful to the individual (this is developed under ten heads, such as "Anatomy of the Soul" and "Directory of Our Duties"), and that "Divine Musick" is useful to society: not only does historical example (Hebrew, early Christian, and Reformation) argue in its favor, but also it contributes to the "Advancement of Piety," the encouragement of literacy, and an increase in church attendance. Chapters III and IV are concerned with the principal reason for the decline of Psalmody, which is lack of support from the "Quality and Gentry." The Old Version is responsible: it is "by the Meanness of the Verse, [that] this Part of Divine Worship has lost its Due Esteem."[27]

In Chapter V Tate surveys some of the difficulties encountered by a new version—ignorance, envy, and disagreements over measures, rhymes, accuracy of translation, and language, whether it should be "Graceful" or "Homely." Chapters VI and VII take up other reasons for Psalmody's decline: the small number of Psalm tunes that some churches actually use, too few either for variety or for the different "Passions" of the Psalms; the general decay of family worship; Psalmody's not being taught in the schools in England, as it is on the Continent; and parish clerks who are poor both in quality and in income. Tate makes the mollifying suggestion that, whatever version is adopted, the profits should be "dispos'd of to the Benefit of Parish-Clerks."[28]

Tate's main thesis, to which he returns again and again, is that an adequate translation of poetry must itself be poetry. In Chapter I he emphasizes that one of the values of the Psalms is their different moods, their "Agreeable Varieties of Style" fitted to their various subjects: most other translators have kept "All upon a Level . . . which Way of Rendering them may be call'd Transforming, but by no Means Translating of the Psalms." In Chapter IV he protests that "Lameness of the Rhimes, Superfluous Words, Homely Phrases, Meanness of the Verse, Barbarity and Botching," all characteristic of the

Old Version, do not characterize the "Sacred Text." And in Chapter V he asks "Is not an Elegant Manner of Translating these Divine Odes, as just a Debt to the Psalmist, as to any Other Poet?"[29]

However, Tate's effort to meet such an objection as that raised by Beveridge is disappointing. Agreeing that ignorant people tend to think that King David wrote the words they recite, Tate tells a story attributed to the Bishop of Ely which shows that the Psalter is sometimes taken in an even more extraordinary way. After instituting Dr. Patrick's metrical version of the Psalms in his own family, the bishop noticed:

> that a Servant-Maid of a Musical Voice, was silent for several Days together. He ask'd her the Reason, whether she were not well, or had a Cold? Adding, that He was much delighted to hear her, because she sang sweetly and kept the Rest in Tune. I am well enough in Health, answer'd she, and have no Cold; but, if you must needs know the plain Truth of the Matter, as long as You sung Jesus Christ's Psalms, I sung along with Ye; but now You sing Psalms of Your Own Invention, You may sing by Your selves.

Tate's solution is the uncomprehending answer of the man who has never really faced the problem of ignorance: "turn to the Title-Page, . . . and shew 'em the Translators Names."[30]

The *New Version* has often been regarded as representing a slackening of religious feeling. However, the reputation of religion in England after 1688 has been improving in recent years,[31] and we have become more aware that it is a mistake to equate striving for elegance with lack of true feeling. From his defense of psalmody it seems clear that Tate thought he was reviving an ailing but very important part of worship that contributed much to the joy of religion; and he referred with enthusiasm to the German example, the "Abundance of Psalms, Hymns, and Spiritual Songs, set to pleasant short Tunes" and the "Heavenly Musick" made by "Peasants at their Plough, their Children and Servants at their Labour, and when they walk in the Fields."[32] Actually, the new day had already come for English hymnody, for Isaac Watts had published his *Hymns and Spiritual Songs* in 1707; twelve years later he would declare his independence of literal translation of the Psalms and have his Psalmist "always speak the common Sense and Language of a Christian."[33] The freer translation and pursuit of style by Tate and Brady in the 1690's, even if it was sometimes a misguided striving for elegance, suggested the direction that hymn-writing would take.

This view is similar to that taken by Louis F. Benson in *The English Hymn,* who places the *New Version* in relation to previous metrical Psalters on the one hand and to the rapid development of the English hymn in the eighteenth century on the other. Benson sees the transition as "proceeding along three lines, more or less synchronous": first, "an effort to improve the literary character of the authorized Psalters"; second, the desire to use the "present language of Christianity" in the Psalms; and, third, the effort to paraphrase portions of the Bible other than the Psalms. The *New Version* was the main development in the first line, and the *Supplement,* which seems to belong chiefly in the third line, "became the actual medium by which hymns were introduced into many churches in and beyond London." "On the whole," Benson feels, "the influence of the *New Version* was very considerable. It set up in the Church of England a new standard of Psalmody, with the same authorization as the older one,—that of a Paraphrase which had something of the freer lyrical spirit of the Hymn as against the restriction of the Metrical Psalm."[34]

In view of the limitations that the translators had to face, it is surprising that the *New Version* is as good as it is. Tate and Brady were restricted by tradition and by form; and they had to make their lines of verse clear, singable, memorable, and elegant—yet not too offensive to those who were accustomed to a more literal translation and to more homely diction. Here, as in so many others of his writings, Tate shows his adaptability, his ingenuity in carrying out a difficult compromise with a considerable degree of success.

CHAPTER 9

A Poem upon Tea

IT IS SOMETIMES SAID that Tate's best poem is *Panacea: A Poem upon Tea: In Two Canto's,* first published in 1700 and republished as *A Poem upon Tea* in 1702.[1] It appeared the year after Dr. Garth's successful mock-heroic poem *The Dispensary,* and it heralded a spate of early eighteenth-century mock-heroic poems on beverages, including John Philips's *Cerealia* (1706) in praise of ale and John Gay's *Wine* (1708).[2] Tate's friend Motteux wrote another *Poem upon Tea* (1712).[3] Although *Panacea* is mock-heroic, the burlesque element is much lighter in Tate's poem than it is in the Miltonic burlesques of Philips and Gay.

I *The Celebration of Tea*

Tea had come to England near the middle of the seventeenth century. At first it was drunk only by the very wealthy, but in 1657 Thomas Garway began underselling the market at his coffeehouse, and tea soon became popular. It was supposed to have many virtues, twenty of which are listed in a manuscript in the British Museum dated 1686 and allegedly translated from the Chinese by Thomas Povey, M. P. The twenty virtues include some that are physical (tea "Prevents the Dropsie" and "Clenseth and Purifieth adult humours and a hot Liver") and some that are mental or ethical (it "Sharpens the Will and Quickens the Understanding" and encourages "the use of due benevolence").[4] In the Preface that Tate added to the second edition of his poem, he observed: "I must honestly acknowledge, 'tis to This (despicable) Tea-

Leaf that I owe Recovery out of a Weakly Constitution from the very Cradle: and make no Doubt of the like Benefit to Others (in most Infirmities) with right Knowledge of this Panacea, and different Preparation and Use of it's Infusion, for the purpose of Pleasure Only, or for Health."

The speaker of Tate's poem is the shepherd Palaemon, who leaves the Avon to visit "Foreign Climates":

> Most strict Survey in every Realm he made
> Of Men and Manners, Policy and Trade;
> But none he found, his gentle Soul to please,
> Like the Refin'd and Civiliz'd Chinese.[5]

On returning home, he introduces his fellow shepherds to tea and then tells his astonished listeners the story of its origin. China had enjoyed a Golden Age until the time of Emperor Ki, who had ruined the country to support his own luxury. He was eventually overthrown, but the diseases that had come with him would not leave. Finally, the new emperor went with his court to consult with Confucius, and growing in front of Confucius's cave they discovered three kinds of tea—Soumblo, Imperial tea, and Bohea—given to Chinamen in compensation for their "Publick Grief." The first canto closes with an announcement of the subject of the second:

> Next, how their [China's] Poets sing (in bolder Verse)
> The Virtues of this Plant—I shall rehearse
> How happily their Art they have Express'd,
> With useful Truth in pleasing Fable drest;
> That sickly Mortals, by the Tempting Lure
> Of Fiction, may be drawn to certain Cure.[6]

In Canto II Palaemon sings the virtues of the plant in terms of a competition among the Goddesses before Jupiter and the "Gods in Council" to see who should be the "Patroness and Guardian" of tea. Speaking first, Juno demands the right to sponsor the "Queen of Plants"; she urges Jove to assert the rights of royalty. Minerva retorts that "Merit" should not give way to "Majesty" and claims the privilege of sponsoring tea for herself in the name of Athens, Isis, and Cam; for tea is especially the reward of scholars, who have surrendered the "Life of Pleasures" to devote themselves to study. It is also the reward of poets:

> From this Pirene, this Castalian Spring,
> Exclude the Muses, And what Muse will sing?
> And when no Poet will vouchsafe to write
> What hardy Hero will vouchsafe to fight[?]
> 'Tis Tea sustains, Tea only can inspire
> The Poet's Flame, that feeds the Hero's Fire.[7]

Venus appeals in the name of Beauty, which, she urges, inspires both soldier and poet; and she points to the tea-drinking British ladies to show the close connection between tea and beauty. Cinthia promptly claims the British ladies (and therefore tea) as her own, for they are particularly famed for their virtue. She is followed by Thetis, who pleads the sea's support of Albion and the tea trade, and then by Salus, the Goddess of Health. Somnus awakens long enough to praise tea as the inspiration of man's happy dreams: "Thus Human Life in cruel Fate's despight, / May have its Sorrows checquered with delight." When the deities quarrel, Jove finally finds the solution in accepting all the goddesses as patronesses of the plant and giving it the name of "Goddess" or "Thea."

At the end of Canto II is "The Tea-Table," a brief poem celebrating tea over strong drink:

> To Bacchus when our Griefs repair for Ease,
> The Remedy proves worse than the Disease:
> Where Reason we must lose to keep the Round,
> And drinking Others Healths, our Own confound:
> Whilst Tea, our Sorrows safely to beguile,
> Sobriety and Mirth does reconcile:
> For to this Nectar we the Blessing owe,
> To grow more Wise, as we more chearful grow.
> Whilst Fancy does her brightest Beams dispense,
> And decent Wit diverts without Offence.
> Then in Discourse of Nature's mystick Pow'rs
> And Noblest Themes, we pass the well-spent Hours.

> Whilst all around the Virtues Sacred Band,
> And list'ning Graces pleas'd Attendants stand.
> Thus our Tea-conversation we employ,
> Where With Delight, Instruction we enjoy;
> Quaffing, without the wast of Time or Wealth,
> The Sov'reign Drink of Pleasure and of Health.

The practical purpose of the poem was supported in the second edition with a handbook for tea drinkers, containing sections headed "An Account of the Nature and Virtues of Tea: With Directions in the Use of It for Health. Collected from Treatises of Learned and Skilful Physicians upon That Subject," "Directions in the Use of Tea," "The several Kinds of Tea," "Observations for Making of Tea," and "For Preserving the Tea-Leaf."

Except for an extravagant dedication to Charles Montague, *A Poem upon Tea* was written without the usual pressures: there was no king or other dignitary to celebrate in heroic verse, no high standard of elegance to strive for, no laureate duty, no musician to satisfy, and no responsibility to sacred text. Tate was able to relax and enjoy imself, and the result is an entertaining poem written with the amused awareness of the relatively trivial nature of his subject that had appeared in such early poems as "Sliding upon Skates."

II *Final Estimate*

In his frequent lack of confidence and vigor, Tate differed from his leading contemporaries, Dryden, Defoe, Swift, and Pope; but in many other respects he was very much of his age. At the same time, his broad literary sympathies linked him with both earlier and later periods, though it is a mistake to think that he belonged more to the other eras than to his own. He combined a Puritan heritage with a modestly successful literary life at the courts of the later Stuarts, William and Mary, and Anne; and his works have affinities with many types of verse and drama from Spenser and Shakespeare to Cibber and Young. As Polonius might say, he wrote verse that is melancholy, moral, panegyrical, satiric, and mock-heroic; and his nine plays and adaptations include at least one in each of the categories of heroic tragedy, sentimental tragedy, history, tragicomedy, realistic comedy, and farce.

Tate also made important contributions to the reestablishment of Shakespeare in the theater, to the early growth of English opera, to the early development of the English hymn, and to the translation of the classics in a style suited to the eighteenth century. He wrote a large number of works, many of which succeeded in their own day, and several of which outlasted the age for which they were written. He was suitably the poet laureate of his time; and, although poverty and failing health seem to have limited his activity after 1702, he carried out what he felt to be the duties of his office with dignity and with responsibility.

Notes and References

Chapter One

1. *A Tale of a Tub,* ed. Herbert Davis (Oxford, 1939), p. 22.

2. Parnell's "Book-Worm" is quoted from *Minor Poets of the Eighteenth Century,* Everymans Library (London, 1930), p. 150. The *Epistle to Dr. Arbuthnot,* 1. 190; *Dunciad* A (1728), I, 103; *Dunciad* B (1743), I, 105 and 238; quoted from the Twickenham Edition, 2nd ed., IV, ed. John Butt, and V, ed. James Sutherland (London and New Haven, 1953).

3. *Johnson on Shakespeare,* ed. Walter Raleigh (London, 1952), pp. 161-62; Sir Walter Scott and George Saintsbury, eds., *The Works of John Dryden* (Edinburgh, 1882), I, 223. According to William Winter, *Shakespeare on the Stage,* Second Series (New York, 1915), p. 366, "Tatefication" was used by Charles Knight; I have found it employed by Henry N. Hudson in his *Lectures on Shakespeare* (New York, 1848), II, 277. For the comments of some of the Romantic critics on *King Lear,* see Chapter IV.

4. Gerard Langbaine, *An Account of the English Dramatick Poets* (Oxford, 1691), p. 500.

5. *Epistle to a Friend concerning Poetry* (London, 1700), reproduced in facsimile in *Series Two: Essays on Poetry,* ed. Edward N. Hooker, The Augustan Reprint Society, No. 2 (Los Angeles, 1947); 11. 702-5 are quoted.

6. *The Cambridge History of English Literature* (Cambridge, England, 1912), VIII, 46.

7. *The Background of Gray's Elegy: A Study in the Taste for Melancholy Poetry 1700-1751* (New York, 1924), p. 66.

8. [T.] Cibber *et al., The Lives of the Poets* (London, 1753), III, 258; David E. Baker, *Biographia Dramatica,* new ed. (London, 1782), I, 443.

9. H. F. Scott-Thomas, "Nahum Tate, Laureate: Two Biographical Notes," *Modern Language Notes,* LVI (1941), 611-12. The works dedicated to physicians are *Poems* (1677); the verse trans-

lation of Fracastoro's *Syphilis* (1686); *An Essay of a Character of . . . Treby* (1699); and *A Congratulatory Poem To . . . Prince George* (1708).

10. "Nahum Tate and the Seventeenth Century," *A Journal of English Literary History,* I (1934), 250-75; p. 272 quoted. Most of this article is from the last chapter of Scott-Thomas's dissertation, "The Life and Works of Nahum Tate" (Johns Hopkins, 1932), 2 vols., although the dissertation is not mentioned in the article.

11. *Ibid.*, p. 255.

12. *Ibid.*, pp. 261, 262.

Chapter Two

1. Samuel A. Golden, "The Three Faithful Teates," *Notes and Queries,* CC (1955), 375. See also Golden's unpublished thesis "Nahum Tate" (Trinity College, Dublin, [1954]), pp. 1-19; St. John D. Seymour, "Faithful Teate," *Journal of the Royal Society of Antiquaries of Ireland,* 6th Series, X (1920), 39-45; and the same author's *The Puritans in Ireland (1647-1661)* (Oxford, 1921), esp. pp. 147-48, 201, 221. The records seem to disagree both about the number of children who died on the journey to Dublin and the number who survived their father.

2. Samuel A. Golden, "Dryden's 'Cleomenes' and Theophilus Parsons," *Notes and Queries,* CCXI (1966), 380, suggests that the Theophilus Parsons whose lines praising *Cleomenes* were published with the play in 1693, "was a first cousin of Nahum Tate."

3. Seymour, *Puritans in Ireland,* p. 201.

4. Golden, "The Three Faithful Teates," p. 378. I have transcribed the title of *Ter Tria* from the second edition (1669).

5. Samuel A. Golden, "Variations in the Name of Nahum Tate," *Notes and Queries,* CCI (1956), 72. Tate's first name was so little known that the author of the lines in defense of Tate in *Commendatory Verses* (London, 1700), p. 14, who used "Nahum" as a rhyme word, added a note explaining that it was "Mr. Tate's Christian Name."

6. Golden, "Nahum Tate," pp. 20-21.

7. "On the Translation of Eutropius, By Young Gentlemen, Educated by Mr. L. Maidwell," *Poems,* 2nd ed. (London, 1684), pp. 217-18.

8. Golden, "Nahum Tate," pp. 21-22.

9. *Ibid.*, p. 23.

10. Quoted from *The Gentleman's Journal* (January-February, 1694), p. 25.

11. Edward MacLysaght, *Irish Life in the Seventeenth Century: After Cromwell* (London, [1939]), pp. 187-89.

12. William S. Clark, *The Early Irish Stage: The Beginnings to 1720* (Oxford, 1955), pp. 49-54, 67-70.

13. The Smock Alley prompt books of Shakespearean plays from the late 1670's and early 1680's are discussed by Clark, pp. 72-77; and by R. C. Bald, "Shakespeare on the Stage in Restoration Dublin," *Publications of the Modern Language Association,* LVI (1941), 369-78; G. Blakemore Evans has included several of the Smock Alley versions in his *Shakespearean Prompt-Books of the Seventeenth Century* (Charlottesville, Virginia, 1960 in progress).

14. See the biography of Flatman in the *Dictionary of National Biography*; Frederic A. Child, *The Life and Uncollected Poems of Thomas Flatman* (Philadelphia, 1921), pp. 5-23; and George Saintsbury's edition of Flatman's poems in *Minor Poets of the Caroline Period* (Oxford, 1921), III.

15. Cotton's copy of *Poems* (1677) is now in the Boston Public Library: see "The Poems of Nahum Tate," *More Books: The Bulletin of the Boston Public Library,* 6th Series, XIII (1938), 152. I am grateful to Mr. John Alden, Keeper of Rare Books, for the information that the licensing date in this copy (on sig. Alv) is November 27, 1676; the leaf is missing in some copies. The second edition of Flatman's *Poems and Songs* was advertised in *The Term Catalogues* for the Michelmas Term (November), 1676; and Tate's *Poems* was advertised for the Hilary Term (February), 1677 (ed. Edward Arber, 3 vols. [London, 1903-6], I, 261, 266-67). Although listing in *The Term Catalogues* does not necessarily mean immediate publication, the probability is that Flatman's and Tate's volumes were published only a few months apart.

16. See the biography of Needham in the *Dictionary of National Biography.*

17. The dates of plays and performances are based upon those given in *The London Stage, 1660-1800,* Part I, 1660-1700, ed. William Van Lennep (Carbondale, Illinois, 1965).

18. Quoted by George R. Noyes, *The Poetical Works of Dryden,* 2nd ed. (Cambridge, Mass., 1950), p. 137, from the fourth edition of *Second Part of Miscellany Poems* (1716).

19. This group is discussed in *The Works of John Dryden,* ed. Edward N. Hooker *et al.* (Berkeley, 1956 in progress), I, 320.

20. Brice Harris, *Charles Sackville, Sixth Earl of Dorset* (Urbana, 1940), esp. pp. 27-28, 35-36, 67-69, 135.

21. See Richard H. Perkinson, "The Polemical Use of Davies'

Nosce Teipsum," *Studies in Philology,* XXXVI (1939), 597-608, esp. 603-8.

22. See P. F. Vernon, "Social Satire in Shadwell's *Timon*," *Studia Neophilologica,* XXXV (1963), 221-26; and Gunnar Sorelius, "Shadwell Deviating into Sense: *Timon of Athens* and the Duke of Buckingham," *Studia Neophilologica,* XXXVI (1964), 232-44.

23. *The London Stage,* Part I, p. 294, suggests that *King Lear* was first performed in March; but James Black, "An Augustan Stage-History: Nahum Tate's *King Lear*," *Restoration and 18th Century Theatre Research,* VI (1967), 36-37, prefers January because of the reference to Tangier in the Epilogue.

24. In his Epistle Dedicatory to *The History of King Richard the Second* (London, 1681), sig. A2v, Tate says that the play was "supprest, first in its own Name, and after in Disguise." However, other documents suggest that it may have been played under two false names, "The Sicilian Usurper" and "The Tyrant of Sicily": see *The London Stage,* Part I, pp. lxiii, 293, 294. Possibly the latter title is simply a misremembered version of the former.

25. John Harold Wilson, "Theatre Notes from the Newdigate Newsletters," *Theatre Notebook,* XV (1961), 80, note.

26. Charles E. Ward, *The Life of John Dryden* (Chapel Hill, 1961), p. 211.

27. *The Term Catalogues,* II, 145.

28. *On the Sacred Memory of Our Late Sovereign: With a Congratulation to His Present Majesty* (London, 1685), p. 6. The first poem in the 1684 volume is "On His Royal Highness's Deliverance from Shipwrack in the *Gloucester,* the Sixth of May, 1682."

29. Scott-Thomas, "Nahum Tate, Laureate: Two Biographical Notes," pp. 611-12.

30. *The Dramatic Works of Sir George Etherege,* ed. H. F. B. Brett-Smith, 2 vols. (Oxford, 1927), I, xxv.

31. For an account of Ashton see David M. Vieth, *Attribution in Restoration Poetry* (New Haven, 1963), pp. 254-70.

32. Carl Niemeyer, "The Earl of Roscommon's Academy," *Modern Language Notes,* XLIX (1934), 432-37. There is advertised on the last page of Tate's *Song for New-Year's Day, 1706,* "Remarques upon the Methods of Education Practised in England, Recommended to the Consideration of Parents, especially of Quality and Gentry," by Tate, but no such work seems to be extant.

33. Golden, "Nahum Tate," pp. 42-44.

34. *The Gentleman's Journal* (October, 1692), p. 17.

35. This work has been published by The Augustan Reprint

Society, No. 51 (Los Angeles, 1955), with an Introduction by J. Max Patrick.

36. *Poems* (1684), p. 168.

37. *Majestas Imperii Britannici. The Glories of Great Britain Celebrated in Latin Poems By Mr. Maidwell. Paraphras'd in English by Mr. Tate,* Part I (London, 1706), sigs. A2v, A3.

38. He is so placed in "Deliverance," published early in February, 1689, and quoted by Sir Walter Scott in his *Life of John Dryden,* ed. Bernard Kreissman (Lincoln, Nebraska, 1963), p. 234, note.

39. For the text of and commentary on the Prologue, published as *The Prolouge* [sic] *to King William and Queen Mary,* see Autrey Nell Wiley, *Rare Prologues and Epilogues 1642-1700* (London, 1940), pp. 273-77.

40. With the revised title the poem was advertised in *The Term Catalogues* in February of 1691 (i.e., 1690/91) and again in February of 1692 (ed. Arber, II, 347, 394).

41. *Ibid.,* II, 333.

42. Parallels with Milton's prose and with "Lycidas" are noted by Scott-Thomas, "Nahum Tate and the Seventeenth Century," pp. 263-66.

43. Quoted from *A Poem Occasioned by the Late Discontents* . . . (London, 1691).

44. The warrant to the attorney or solicitor general is dated December 8: *Calendar of State Papers, Domestic Series,* 1691-92 (London, 1900), p. 519. See also Edmund K. Broadus, *The Laureateship* (Oxford, 1921), p. 89.

45. *The Gentleman's Journal* (November, 1692), p. 22. This issue was actually published in December, for Motteux also referred to the death of William Mountfort on December 9.

46. *Calendar of Treasury Books,* 1685-89, Vol. VIII, Part I, p. 139. See also Louis I. Bredvold, "Notes on John Dryden's Pension," *Modern Philology,* XXX (1932), 268-69.

47. *Calendar of Treasury Books,* 1689-92, Vol. IX, Part V (London, 1931), p. 1950, dated December 23, 1692. Rymer's patent "with all the rights, advantages etc. thereto, as amply as Thomas Shadwell or any other predecessor therein: with an annuity or yearly pension of £200" is recorded under the same date on p. 1969.

48. The request appears in the *Calendar of State Papers, Domestic Series,* 1699-1700 (London, 1937), p. 372, dated February 5, 1700. The grant can be traced from February to early April in the *Calendar of Treasury Books,* XV (London, 1933), pp. 51, 52, 290, 315.

49. Broadus, *The Laureateship,* p. 62 and Appendix I, pp. 219-22.

50. *Majestas Imperii Britannici,* sig. A2.

51. *The Post Angel,* April, 1701, p. 299, cited by Scott-Thomas, "Life and Works of Nahum Tate," p. 1.

52. According to Hugh Macdonald, *John Dryden, A Bibliography of Early Editions and Drydeniana* (Oxford, 1939), p. 53, the translation of Juvenal was advertised in *The London Gazette* for October 24-27, 1692.

53. See the biography of Collier in the *Dictionary of National Biography.*

54. I quote from microfilm of the original. Joseph Wood Krutch, *Comedy and Conscience after the Restoration,* rev. ed. (New York, 1949), pp. 177-78, quotes the entire letter.

55. Cavendish Weedon, *The Oration, Anthems and Poems* (London, [1702]), sig. A2, p. 8.

56. Richard C. Boys, *Sir Richard Blackmore and the Wits,* University of Michigan Contributions in Modern Philology, No. 13 (Ann Arbor, 1949), p. 6, note, gives the date.

57. *Ibid.,* pp. 37, 95-96, 134-35. The poems are quoted from *Commendatory Verses* (London, 1700), p. 14, and *Discommendatory Verses* (London, 1700), also p. 14. W. J. Cameron, "The Authorship of 'Commendatory Verses,' 1700," *Notes and Queries,* CCVIII (1963), 63, agrees that the defense of Tate was probably by Brady.

58. James Sutherland, *Defoe,* 2nd ed. (London, 1950), pp. 69-74, 286; William Ogg, *England in the Reigns of James II and William III* (Oxford, 1955), pp. 462-64. Tate's poem was advertised in *The Term Catalogues* for February and for May, 1701 (ed. Arber, III, 231, 244).

59. Tate's contribution to the four-volume translation of Lucian published in 1710-11 is in Vol. IV, pp. 233-83. Since it is said in the Dedication in Vol. I that some of the translations were "done before and in the year 1696," and since the translation of Lucian is presumably that mentioned in *The Gentleman's Journal* for June, 1693 (p. 195) and March, 1694 (p. 63), Tate's work may date from the reign of William. On this translation see Hardin Craig, "Dryden's Lucian," *Classical Philology,* XVI (1921), 141-63.

60. These figures are from Gregory King's estimates for 1688; they are given in G. N. Clark, *The Later Stuarts 1660-1714* (Oxford, 1934), p. 25.

61. Samuel A. Golden, "The Late Seventeenth Century Writer

and the Laureateship: Nahum Tate's Tenure," *Hermathena*, LXXXIX (May, 1957), 30-38. See the *Calendar of Treasury Books*, XVIII, 225; XIX, 60; XX, 229; XXVI, 33, 270.

62. An analysis of the agreement appears in *The Gentleman's Magazine*, Vol. XCII, Part II (1822), 414-16; Henry A. Glass, *The Story of the Psalters* (London, 1888), p. 108, refers to the document also, but adds that "the property . . . very soon after vested in the Stationers' Company."

63. *Memoirs of the Mint and Queen's-Bench, . . . with . . . a Poem to the Marshall by Mr. Tate* (London, 1713).

64. On Carlisle see Scott-Thomas, "Nahum Tate, Laureate: Two Biographical Notes," pp. 611-12; the elegy for Queen Anne closes with flattery of Buckingham.

65. Morris Freedman, "Dryden's 'Memorable Visit' to Milton," *Huntington Library Quarterly*, XVIII (1955), 99-108, is an excellent article on the visit, but Freedman has little to say of *The Monitor's* account, which, I think, may well have come to *The Monitor* through Tate from Dryden.

66. Smith is quoted from his Preface to the second edition of *An Entire Set of the Monitors* (London, [1715?]). Scott-Thomas, "The Life and Works of Nahum Tate," I, 259; II, 233-35, points out that eight of the poems had appeared in the second edition of Tate's *Poems* (1684). He also says that one poem of the apparent total of forty-one is a fragment of another and that therefore there are really only forty; however, if the introductory address to the queen, which is in verse, is included in the count, there are still forty-one. Probably more than eight of the poems are by Tate: as Hoxie N. Fairchild, *Religious Trends in English Poetry*, I, 1700-40 (New York, 1939), 178, remarks, "most of them . . . sound very much like" Tate.

67. H. F. Scott-Thomas, "The Date of Nahum Tate's Death," *Modern Language Notes*, XLIX (1934), 169-71.

68. Broadus, *The Laureateship*, p. 106.

69. The "gentleman" is not identified, and the papers are not known to have survived. Tate's elegy was also published as the first poem in *The Loyal Mourner for the Best of Princes: Being a Collection of Poems Sacred to the Immortal Memory of Her Late Majesty Queen Anne* (London and Dublin, 1716), edited by Charles Oldisworth. Oldisworth (sig. A3v) calls Tate's poem "the last and best that ever he wrote."

Chapter Three

1. Reed, *The Background of Gray's Elegy,* p. 27; Draper, *The Funeral Elegy and the Rise of English Romanticism* (New York, 1929).
2. "On the Death of my Dear Brother Mr. Richard Flatman," *Poems and Songs,* 4th ed. (London, 1686), p. 193.
3. *Poems,* 2nd ed. (1684), pp. 11-12.
4. *Ibid.,* pp. 64-65.
5. *Ibid.,* pp. 101-2. The resemblance to Young (and the resemblance to Arnold in the next example) are pointed out by Scott-Thomas, "The Life and Works of Nahum Tate," I, 325, 327.
6. *Poems,* 2nd ed., p. 76.
7. *Ibid.,* p. 81. In the list of errata (sig. A7v), the misprint "Honour" is corrected to "Humour."
8. *Ibid.,* pp. 56-64.
9. This poem is quoted from the first edition of *Poems* (1677), pp. 14-15. It was heavily revised in the second edition, although the only revision of significance in the lines quoted was the unfortunate substitution of "(alas too prone.) contriving" for "endeav'ring" in the fourth line. Scott-Thomas, "The Life and Works of Nahum Tate," I, 9, says that Dryden admired this poem, but he gives no evidence for his statement.
10. *The Influence of Milton on English Poetry* (Cambridge, Mass., 1922), p. 566, and note, where he quotes Tate's poem in full. Tate's use of the phrase "Wood-wild Notes" in "To the Athenian Society" (cf. Milton's "L'Allegro," l. 134, "wood-notes wild") seems to have been first noticed by George Sherburn in "The Early Popularity of Milton's Minor Poems," *Modern Philology,* XVII (1919), 522.
11. *Poems,* 2nd ed., p. 83.
12. Complimentary verses by Tate accompanying Francis Fane's *The Sacrifice* (London, 1686).
13. *Poems,* 2nd ed., pp. 31-32.
14. *Ibid.,* p. 105.
15. *Ibid.,* p. 69.
16. Scott-Thomas, "The Life and Works of Nahum Tate," I, 330, points out the resemblance of "The Hurricane" to *The Tempest.*
17. *Ibid.,* I, 332-36; II, 205-33, includes many examples of Tate's revisions for the second edition.
18. *Poems* (1677), p. 27; *Poems,* 2nd ed., p. 28.
19. *Poems,* 2nd ed., pp. 153-54.

20. *Works of John Dryden,* ed. Hooker, I, 324; Ward, *Life of John Dryden,* p. 143.

21. *Essays of John Dryden,* ed. W. P. Ker (Oxford, 1926), I, 236.

22. *Ibid.,* p. 255.

23. *Works of John Dryden,* ed. Hooker, I, 326-28.

24. The text of the *Second Part of Absalom and Achitophel* that I have used is the one in the second edition of Noyes's *Poetical Works of Dryden.*

25. *Essays,* ed. Ker, II, 9. The estimate was made by David Nichol Smith, *John Dryden* (Cambridge, England, 1950), p. 68.

26. *Ovid's Metamorphosis. Translated by Several Hands,* Vol. I (London, 1697), sig. A6.

27. *Letters of John Dryden,* ed. Charles E. Ward (Durham, N.C., 1942), pp. 50, 162. See also Macdonald, *John Dryden,* p. 67, note.

28. *Ovid's Metamorphosis,* I (1697), sig. A7.

29. *Juvenal the Satirist* (Oxford, 1954), p. 214.

30. *Clarissa* (Oxford, 1930), IV, 339.

31. Ward, *Life of John Dryden,* p. 364.

32. *Juvenal and Persius,* tr. G. G. Ramsay, rev. ed. (Cambridge, Mass., 1950), pp. 17-19.

33. *The Satires of Decimus Junius Juvenalis. Translated into English Verse. By Mr. Dryden and Several Other Eminent Hands* (London, 1693), p. 19.

34. *Essays,* ed. Ker, I, 237.

35. *The Gentleman's Journal* (November, 1693), pp. 380-82.

Chapter Four

1. *The Historia Regum Britanniae of Geoffrey of Monmouth,* ed. Acton Griscom (London, 1929), pp. 225-28, 259-60.

2. The principal source of *Locrine* was probably Geoffrey of Monmouth; on the sources and on Assaracus, see Baldwin Maxwell, *Studies in the Shakespeare Apocrypha* (New York, 1956), pp. 27ff., 41. Scott-Thomas, "The Life and Works of Nahum Tate," I, 58-59, tries to find other parallels between Tate's play and *Locrine;* but those he points out are not striking. Ernest Jones, *Geoffrey of Monmouth 1648-1800* (Berkeley, 1944), p. 407, says that in Tate's play "there is no faintest hint of Geoffrey."

3. On the edition of Shakespeare's play used in *The Ingratitude of a Common-Wealth,* see Ruth E. McGugan, "Nahum Tate and

the Coriolanus Tradition in English Drama with a Critical Edition of Tate's *The Ingratitude of a Common-Wealth,"* unpublished dissertation (University of Illinois, 1965), pp. lviii-lix. On *King Lear* see Hazelton Spencer, *Shakespeare Improved* (Cambridge, Mass., 1927), pp. 250 and 273; and Christopher Spencer, *Five Restoration Adaptations of Shakespeare* (Urbana, Ill., 1965), pp. 442-43. On *Richard II* see H. Spencer, p. 262 (where he favors Q5 as the source), but also p. 273, note 13. *Locrine* was still being published in 1734 with Shakespeare's name on the title page: two such editions are listed in *The British Museum General Catalogue of Printed Books,* CCXX (London, 1964), col. 356.

4. T. D. Kendrick, *British Antiquity* (London, 1950), pp. 101-2.
5. *Brutus of Alba* (London, 1678), p. 25. Cf. *Macbeth,* I.iii.7ff.
6. *Brutus of Alba,* p. 27.
7. *Charles Lamb's Specimens of English Dramatic Poets,* ed. Israel Gollancz (London, 1893), II, 301-4.
8. *Brutus of Alba,* pp. 25-26, 47-48.
9. *Ibid.,* pp. 15, 18, 19.
10. *Ibid.,* pp. 56-[57].
11. *Ibid.,* p. 49.
12. *Ibid.,* p. 28.
13. [John Genest], *Some Account of the English Stage, from the Restoration in 1660 to 1830* (Bath, 1832), II, 79-81; and *The London Stage,* Part I, p. 468.
14. (New York, 1951), p. 42.
15. Ed. Imogen Holst (London, 1959), pp. 3, 34, 36, 40.
16. (Cambridge, Mass., 1961), pp. 41, 59ff.
17. I quote from the facsimile of the unique copy of the printed edition of the libretto in the Royal College of Music, in the Purcell Society edition of *The Works of Henry Purcell,* III (London, 1889).
18. Moore, p. 41, note.
19. Eric W. White, "Early Theatrical Performances of Purcell's Operas," *Theatre Notebook,* XIII (1958-59), p. 43.
20. Described by White, "New Light on 'Dido and Aeneas'" in Holst, ed., *Henry Purcell,* pp. 15-17.
21. This version of *Measure for Measure* is described in some detail by H. Spencer, *Shakespeare Improved,* pp. 329-35. White discusses the mask and prints the new passage in Act II in "New Light on 'Dido and Aeneas'"; and W. M. Merchant comments on the mask in relation to the play in "Shakespeare 'Made Fit'" in *Stratford-upon-Avon Studies,* No. 6, *Restoration Theatre* (London, 1965), pp. 216-18.

22. White, "New Light on 'Dido and Aeneas,'" pp. 27-28.
23. White, "Early Theatrical Performances of Purcell's Operas," p. 48.
24. *The Loyal General* (London, 1680), p. 2.
25. *Ibid.*, pp. 9, 24, 29.
26. *Ibid.*, pp. 45-46.
27. "The Life and Works of Nahum Tate," I, 85. See *Henry IV, Part II*, III.i.4-31. Tate's quoting from *Henry VI, Part III* in his dedication suggests that he might also have been influenced by Henry's laments in II.v of that play.
28. Some of the ideas in this and successive paragraphs also appeared in my "A Word for Tate's *King Lear*," *Studies in English Literature 1500-1900*, III (1963), 241-51, and in the Introduction to my *Five Restoration Adaptations of Shakespeare*.
29. Quoted from *Gray's-Inn Journal* (1754), II, 222, by H. H. Furness, ed., *King Lear*, New Variorum Edition (Philadelphia, 1880), p. 478.
30. [Francis Gentleman], *The Dramatic Censor* (London, 1770), I, 377.
31. Addison's comment appears in *The Spectator*, No. 40 (April 16, 1711); in context Addison is arguing against poetic justice, possibly with his own tragedy *Cato* in mind. Coleman's version is described and his advertisement is quoted at length by Genest, *Some Account of the English Stage*, V, 191-203.
32. Quoted from *The Examiner* for May 22, 1808, by Lawrence H. and Carolyn W. Houtchens, *Leigh Hunt's Dramatic Criticism 1808-1831* (New York, 1949), pp. 15-17. Lamb's comments are in his essay "On the Tragedies of Shakspere" (1811).
33. *Shakespearean Tragedy*, 2nd ed. (London, 1905), pp. 251-54.
34. There is a good discussion of Tate's adaptation and especially of the Dedication in W. M. Merchant's "Shakespeare 'Made Fit,'" pp. 195-200, 211-13. The Dedication is addressed to a friend, Thomas Boteler. Montague Summers, ed. *Shakespeare Adaptations* (Boston, 1922), p. 280, identifies Boteler as "of the family of the Duke of Ormond"; and Ayres, "Shakespeare in the Restoration," unpublished dissertation (Ohio State University, 1964), p. 28, further identifies him as the son of Robert Butler of London, born in 1652 (like Tate) and mentioned in two of Ormond's letters. On the other hand, Arthur H. Scouten, "Aston Cokain and His Adapter Nahum Tate," unpublished dissertation (Louisiana State University, 1942), p. cxii and note, identifies Boteler as a cousin

of Aston Cokain, whose *Trappolin Suppos'd a Prince* Tate was soon to adapt.

35. George Winchester Stone, Jr., "Garrick's Production of *King Lear*," *Studies in Philology*, XLV (1948), 97-98, also compares Tate's and Shakespeare's versions of Edmund's soliloquy.

36. This and other quotations from Tate's *King Lear* are from my *Five Restoration Adaptations of Shakespeare*.

37. W. M. Merchant, *Shakespeare and the Artist* (London, 1959), p. 24.

38. *Cambridge History of English Literature*, VIII, 46.

Chapter Five

1. John Pollock, *The Popish Plot* (London, 1903), p. 103. Among the many discussions of the plot and the exclusion crisis, I have found two especially useful: David Ogg, *England in the Reign of Charles II*, 2nd ed. (Oxford, 1956), 559-619; and Francis S. Ronalds, *The Attempted Whig Revolution of 1678-1681* (Urbana, Ill., 1937).

2. Address "To the Reader" in Edward Ravenscroft, *Titus Andronicus* (London, 1687). Although the adaptation was not published until 1687, Ravenscroft says that "it first appear'd upon the Stage, at the beginning of the pretended Popish Plot."

3. John Crowne, *The Misery of Civil War* (London, 1680), p. 36. On the influence of politics on the drama during this period, see George W. Whiting, "Political Satire in London Stage Plays, 1680-83," *Modern Philology*, XXVIII (1930), 29-43; and the second chapter of John Loftis, *The Politics of Drama in Augustan England* (Oxford, 1963).

4. See E. K. Chambers, *William Shakespeare: A Study of Facts and Problems* (Oxford, 1930), I, 353-55; II, 323-27. There is a useful discussion of this material in Peter Ure's Introduction to the New Arden edition of *Richard II* (London, 1956), pp. lvii-lxii.

5. Howard's book is discussed by H. J. Oliver, *Sir Robert Howard (1626-1698)* (Durham, N.C., 1963), pp. 242-46.

6. *Shakespeare from Betterton to Irving* (New York, 1920), I, 57.

7. *The History of King Richard the Second* (London, 1681), sigs. A-A1v. The Epistle is addressed to George Raynsford, Esq.

8. *Ibid.*, sig. A2v.

9. Both sets of names are given in the list of characters.

10. *Ibid.*, sigs. A1v, A2.
11. *Ibid.*, p. 26.
12. *Ibid.*, pp. 38-39.
13. *Ibid.*, pp. 13-15.
14. *Ibid.*, p. 20.
15. *Ibid.*, pp. 53-54.
16. *Holinshed's Chronicles of England, Scotland, and Ireland* (London, 1808), III, 13-14.
17. *The History of King Richard the Second,* pp. 31, 37-40, 47-50.
18. *Shakespeare from Betterton to Irving,* I, 58.
19. *The History of King Richard the Second,* p. 6.
20. *Ibid.*, p. 12.
21. *Ibid.*, p. 11.
22. *Ibid.*, p. 51.
23. *Ibid.*, p. 20.
24. *Ibid.*, pp. 22-24.
25. *Ibid.*, sig. A3.
26. Macdonald, *John Dryden,* p. 20, gives the date of Dryden's poem. On the date of *The Ingratitude* see *The London Stage,* Part I, pp. 303-4.
27. *The Ingratitude of a Common-Wealth* (London, 1682), sigs. A2-A2v.
28. In the four Folios of Shakespeare's plays and the Quarto of 1691, there were act divisions but no scene divisions or locations. Rowe provided the scene divisions and some locations in 1709, and others were supplied by other editors during the eighteenth century. Those given here are from G. B. Harrison, ed., *Shakespeare: The Complete Works* (New York, 1952).
29. The three stage directions quoted at length are from *The Ingratitude of a Common-Wealth,* pp. 17, 38, 46.
30. *Ibid.*, p. 27.
31. *Samuel Johnson on Shakespeare,* ed. W. K. Wimsatt (New York, 1960), p. 105.
32. *The Ingratitude of a Common-Wealth,* pp. 62-63.
33. *Ibid.*, p. 9.
34. *Samuel Johnson on Shakespeare,* p. 105.
35. *The History of King Richard the Second,* sig. A; *The Ingratitude of a Common-Wealth,* sig. A2.
36. Macdonald, *John Dryden,* p. 31.
37. *Poems,* 2nd ed., sig. A2v.
38. David Ogg, *England in the Reigns of James II and Wil-*

liam III (Oxford, 1955), pp. 139-40.

39. Quotations from *The Second Part of Absalom and Achitophel* are from Noyes, *The Poetical Works of Dryden,* pp. 137-52.

40. Noyes points out some imitations and borrowings in his notes. "Till peace itself is war in masquerade" (1. 269) is 1. 752 of the first part, with "Till" substituted for "And."

41. On the relation of the first part to Milton's epics, see Morris Freedman, "Dryden's Miniature Epic," *Journal of English and Germanic Philology,* LVII (1958), 211-19.

42. For Tonson, see Chapter II, note 18, above. Scott is quoted from the Scott-Saintsbury edition of *The Works of John Dryden,* IX, 321.

Chapter Six

1. Leo Hughes, "The Early Career of *Farce* in the Theatrical Vocabulary," University of Texas *Studies in English,* 1940, pp. 82-95.

2. *Works of John Dryden,* ed. Hooker, I, 365-66.

3. *Essays of John Dryden,* ed. Ker, I, 135-36.

4. *The Gentleman's Journal* (January, 1693), p. 28.

5. The Preface is not in Ker's selection. I quote from the Scott-Saintsbury edition of *The Works of John Dryden,* VIII, 219.

6. William S. Clark, ed., *The Dramatic Works of Roger Boyle, Earl of Orrery* (Cambridge, Mass., 1937), II, 958-59, says that *Guzman* was licensed on October 27, 1692, and advertised in the *London Gazette* on March 9-13, 1693. *A Duke and No Duke* was advertised in *The Term Catalogues* in May (ed. Arber, II, 454), though it was referred to in January (see note 4).

7. It was advertised in *The Term Catalogues* in November, 1684 (ed. Arber, II, 98), although it was published with 1685 on the title page. The Prologue and Epilogue were published separately in 1684.

8. On Tate and Mariscotti's *De Personis et Larvis, earumque; apud Veteres usu, & Origine, Syntagmation,* see A. H. Scouten, "An Italian Source for Nahum Tate's Defence of Farce," *Italica,* XXVII (1950), 238-40; and Samuel A. Golden, "An Early Defense of Farce" in *Studies in Honor of John Wilcox,* ed. A. D. Wallace and W. O. Ross (Detroit, 1958), pp. 61-70; on p. 70, note 7, Golden mentions the 1691 edition.

9. *A Duke and No Duke,* 2nd ed. (London, 1693), sig. C2.

10. *Ibid.,* sig. C2v.

11. *Ibid.*, sigs. B4v-C, C2v-C3.

12. Leo Hughes, *A Century of English Farce* (Princeton, 1956), pp. 18-19, quoted with approval from the *Encylopaedia Britannica,* 11th ed., "Farce."

13. *A Preface to Restoration Drama* (Boston, 1956), p. 132.

14. *Character and Conflict: An Introduction to Drama* (New York, 1963), p. 748.

15. "Introduction: The Psychology of Farce" in *Let's Get a Divorce! and Other Plays* (New York, 1958), pp. ix-x.

16. Gerald E. Bentley, *The Jacobean and Caroline Stage,* III (Oxford, 1956), 171-72, thinks it was performed before 1642; James Maidment and W. H. Logan, eds., *The Dramatic Works of Aston Cokain* (Edinburgh, 1874), p. 117, think that it was performed both before and after the Restoration; Leo Hughes and A. H. Scouten, eds., *Ten English Farces* (Austin, Texas, 1948), pp. 4-5, note, seem skeptical that it was performed at all.

17. Kathleen M. Lea, "Sir Aston Cokayne and the 'Commedia dell' Arte,'" *Modern Language Review,* XXIII (1928), 47-51. Cokain's statements are made in the Prologue and Epilogue of *Trappolin.*

18. Scouten, "Aston Cokain and His Adapter Nahum Tate," p. cxxxv.

19. Trappolin is so described in the list of characters. I quote the play itself from Hughes and Scouten, eds., *Ten English Farces,* which does not include the 1693 Preface.

20. *Ibid.,* p. 4.

21. *Ibid.,* p. 23.

22. Genest, *Some Account of the English Stage,* I, 440, points this out.

23. Hughes and Scouten, p. 34. This passage is not in Cokain.

24. *Ibid.,* p. 15.

25. *Ibid.,* p. 25. These lines are based upon some in Cokain: see *The Dramatic Works of Sir Aston Cokain,* pp. 177, 179.

26. Scouten, "Aston Cokain and His Adapter Nahum Tate," pp. cxl-cxlvi.

27. Hughes and Scouten, pp. 4-7. *The London Stage,* Part IV, Vol. I, pp. 373, 410, lists it as an afterpiece for *King Lear,* advertised but not given on May 23, 1753, and given on February 18, 1754, both at Drury Lane.

28. *Cuckolds-Haven* (London, 1685), sig. A.

29. *Ibid.,* sig. Alv.

30. C. H. Herford and Percy and Evelyn Simpson, eds., *Ben*

Jonson, VI (Oxford, 1938), 241 (IV.iv.170-71).

31. Julia H. Harris, ed., *Eastward Hoe* (New Haven, 1926), p. 141, describes Cuckolds Haven as "about 2½ miles as the crow flies" below London Bridge.

32. *The First Modern Comedies* (Cambridge, Mass., 1959), p. 217.

33. *Shakespeare Adaptations* (Boston, 1922), p. lxxxiii.

34. *The London Stage,* Part I, p. cxxviii.

35. Arthur Colby Sprague, *Beaumont and Fletcher on the Restoration Stage* (New York, 1965; first published 1926), pp. 137-54.

36. Helen McAfee, *Pepys on the Restoration Stage* (New York, 1965; first published 1916), p. 89 (January 7, 1669).

37. Sprague, *Beaumont and Fletcher on the Restoration Stage,* p. 138.

38. *Ibid.,* p. 267.

39. *The Island-Princess* (London, 1687), p. 42.

40. "Nahum Tate," p. 259.

41. *The London Stage,* Part I, p. 357.

42. *The Island-Princess,* sig. A2.

43. McAfee, *Pepys on the Restoration Stage,* pp. 129-30 (October 2, 1661; November 2, 1666; November 25, 1668).

44. Earl R. Wasserman, *Elizabethan Poetry in the Eighteenth Century* (Urbana, Ill., 1947), p. 30, points this out. See note 73 of Fielding's play (G. H. Nettleton and A. E. Case, eds., *British Dramatists from Dryden to Sheridan* [Boston, 1939], p. 590); and *Injur'd Love* (London, 1707), p. 34.

45. Hazelton Spencer, "Tate and *The White Devil,*" *A Journal of English Literary History,* I (1934), 249.

46. *Injur'd Love,* p. 7.

47. H. Spencer, "Tate and *The White Devil,*" p. 242. Clifford Leech, *John Webster* (London, 1951), pp. 15-19, also comments on Tate's adaptation and points out some inconsistencies.

48. *Injur'd Love,* p. 15.

49. *The Island-Princess,* sigs. A3v-A4.

Chapter Seven

1. Henry L. Clarke, "John Blow: A Tercentenary Survey," *Musical Quarterly,* XXXV (1949), 415.

2. John Dennis, "The Grounds of Criticism in Poetry," 1704, in Willard H. Durham, ed., *Critical Essays of the Eighteenth Century, 1700-1725* (New Haven, 1915), p. 195.

3. Epistle Dedicatory to "A Poem on the Late Promotion of Several Eminent Persons" in *Funeral Poems* (London, 1700), sig. H4.

4. Reed, *The Background of Gray's Elegy,* p. 77.

5. "A Classical Education and Eighteenth-Century Poetry," *Scrutiny,* VIII (1939), 193, 207. See also K. G. Hamilton's chapter "Poetry and Rhetoric" in *The Two Harmonies* (Oxford, 1963), pp. 45-94.

6. (London, 1708), sig. A1v.

7. Van Doren, *John Dryden,* 3rd ed., p. 52. Dryden's theory and practice is discussed by Jean H. Hagstrum in Chapter VII of *The Sister Arts* (Chicago, 1958).

8. *Essays of John Dryden,* ed. Ker, II, 125.

9. (London, 1703), sig. A3v.

10. *Ibid.,* p. 14.

11. First published in 1695; quoted from *Funeral Poems,* p. 1.

12. *A Poem Sacred to the Glorious Memory of Her Late Majesty Queen Anne* (London, 1716), p. 7. In the second line "Cow'r" is an ink emendation of "Low'r" in the British Museum copy 11631.e.63.

13. *A Pastoral Elegy on the Death of Mr. John Playford* (London, 1687). Although it has been suggested that this elegy was written for the younger John Playford, who died aged twenty-one (see Zimmerman, *Henry Purcell,* p. 211), it seems more likely to be for the father, as is assumed by Frank Kidson, "John Playford, and 17th-Century Music Publishing," *Musical Quarterly,* IV (1918), 529.

14. *On The Sacred Memory of Our Late Sovereign: with a Congratulation to His Present Majesty* (London, 1685), p. 3.

15. First published in 1688 without the Latin title, which was used in *Elegies* (London, 1699) and *Funeral Poems.* In 1688 the speakers were named Clotin and Hubbal.

16. "An Elegy in Memory of That Most Excellent Lady The Late Countess of Dorset. Written in the Year, 1691." Apparently, it was not published separately but appeared in several collections, including *The Temple of Death, A Poem,* 2nd ed. (London, 1695), where a much shorter version of the elegy was used, and Tate's *Elegies* and *Funeral Poems*; I quote from the last, pp. [65]-79.

17. *An Elegy on the Most Reverend Father in God, His Grace, John, Late Lord Archbishop of Canterbury,* first published in 1695; quoted from *Funeral Poems,* where it is incorrectly dated 1693, pp. 27-42.

18. *A Consolatory Poem To the Right Honourable John Lord*

Cutts, first published in 1698; quoted from *Funeral Poems,* pp. [81]-100. The print is mentioned in the *Dictionary of National Biography,* V, 369.

19. "Anacharsis; Or the Exercises of Youth" in *The Works of Lucian, Translated from the Greek by Several Eminent Hands* (London, 1710-11), IV, 142-71. Craig, "Dryden's Lucian," p. 162, identifies J. Washington as the "author of a well-known *Abridgement of the Statutes of King William and Queen Mary and of King William III*" and gives his dates as 1688-1707. That he did not live until 1707 is also shown by the fact that the *Abridgment,* listed in *The Term Catalogues* in November, 1694 (the same month as Tate's elegy was licensed), was listed in June, 1699, as "continued after [Washington's] Death" to 1696 (ed. Arber, II, 523; III, 137).

20. *In Memory of Joseph Washington, Esq; Late of the Middle Temple, An Elegy* (London, 1694), p. 4.

21. *An Elegy in Memory of the Much Esteemed and truly Worthy Ralph Marshall, Esq;* (London, 1700), sig. A2, p. 3.

22. *The Diary of John Evelyn,* Everymans Library ed. (London, 1907), II, 364 (December 8, 1700).

23. *An Essay of a Character Of the Right Honourable Sir George Treby* (London, 1699); *A Monumental Poem in Memory of The Right Honourable Sir George Treby Kt. . . . Consisting of His Character and Elegy* (London, 1702).

24. *The Muse's Bower, An Epithalamium* (London, 1713), p. 5.

25. Presumably, Tate published the poem soon after the marriage in December, 1712, and before the bride's death in November, 1713 (see the *Dictionary of National Biography,* VIII, 1289). Pope's revisions of *The Rape of the Lock* were finished by December 8, 1713; and the revised edition of the poem was published on March 2, 1714 (Twickenham ed., II, ed. Geoffrey Tillotson, 2nd ed. [New Haven, 1954], 103-4).

26. *The Muse's Bower,* p. 6.

27. *Dictionary of National Biography,* XIV, 1185-86.

28. *The Muse's Bower,* p. 6.

29. *Ibid.*

30. E. K. Broadus, "The Laureateship," *The London Mercury,* XXII (1930), 134; *The Laureateship,* pp. 80, 91, 102.

31. *The London Stage,* Part I, p. 516. Broadus, *The Laureateship,* p. 91, note, says that he found five birthday odes and six New Year odes by Tate, but he does not give their dates.

32. *The Gentleman's Journal* (January-February, 1694), p. 25.

33. *The Anniversary Ode for . . . His Majesty's Birth-Day. Another for New-Year's-Day* (London, 1698), sig. A2.
34. "Neo-Classical Criticism of the Ode for Music," *Publications of the Modern Language Association,* LXII (1947), 411-21.
35. Zimmerman, *Henry Purcell,* No. 321.
36. *Ode upon Her Majesty's Birth-Day* (London, 1693).
37. Myers, p. 412.
38. (London, 1706). It is also in Tate's paraphrase of Maidwell's Latin poems, *Majestas Imperii Britannici.*
39. (London, 1705), sig. A2, pp. 4-5.
40. George N. Shuster, *The English Ode from Milton to Keats* (New York, 1940), pp. 6, 50-53.

Chapter Eight

1. Henry A. Glass, *The Story of the Psalters* (London, 1888), p. 10.
2. John Julian, ed., *A Dictionary of Hymnology* (London, 1907), p. 928. Glass comments on about one hundred and twenty *complete* versions of the Psalms made between 1549 and 1885 and gives the first verses of Psalms 1 and 23 for each.
3. "English Metrical Psalms in the Sixteenth Century and Their Literary Significance," *Huntington Library Quarterly,* IX (1946), 249-71.
4. Glass, pp. 29-31, 74-75.
5. The Old Version is quoted from the 1696 edition of *The Whole Book of Psalms* printed in London by W. and J. Wilde in order to include the revisions that had been made by Tate's day.
6. *Essays,* ed. Ker, I, 199.
7. The *New Version* is quoted from *A New Version of the Psalms of David* (London, 1712), the last edition published during Tate's life that is listed in the *British Museum General Catalogue of Printed Books,* XVII (London, 1965), col. 792.
8. See the life of Erady in *The Dictionary of National Biography.*
9. In Julian, ed., p. 919.
10. Golden, "Nahum Tate," p. 171, refers to the publication of five Psalms but does not mention the edition of eight. I have seen two "editions" of 1696 at the British Museum, which seem to differ only in the arrangement of the front matter.
11. Both the king's approval and the bishop's recommendation are normally printed in the front of the *New Version.*

12. Julian, ed., pp. 799-800.

13. *Ibid.*, p. 801. Although Julian says he has not seen an edition of the *Supplement* published before 1702, there is an edition dated 1700 in the British Museum; it is bound with an edition of the Psalms dated 1699, and is advertised at the end of that edition.

14. The queen's approval was printed with the *Supplement.*

15. "On Sternhold and Hopkins, and the new Version of David's Psalms," Tom Brown, *Works,* 7th ed. (London, 1730), IV, 64.

16. Henry W. Foote, *Three Centuries of American Hymnody* (Cambridge, Mass., 1940), pp. 38, 60.

17. Golden, "Nahum Tate," p. 181.

18. On the hymn tunes see *Hymns Ancient and Modern,* Historical Edition (London, 1909); and the Introduction in Robert G. McCutchan, *Hymn Tune Names* (New York, 1957).

19. C. S. Phillips, *Hymnody Past and Present* (London, 1937), p 145. On the discussions of music, see Herbert M. Schueller, "The Use and Decorum of Music as Described in British Literature," *Journal of the History of Ideas,* XIII (1952), pp. 88-89 and note.

20. Quotations from the Prayer Book version of the Psalms are from *The Book of Common Prayer* (Cambridge, England: John Hayes, 1673).

21. *Church-Musick Vindicated. A Sermon Preach'd At St. Bride's Church, on Monday November 22, 1697* (London, 1697), pp. 6-7.

22. A. B. Grosart in his life of Beveridge in the *Dictionary of National Biography,* II, 447.

23. *A Defence of the Book of Psalms* (London, 1710), pp. 2, 3, 60-61.

24. *Ibid.*, pp. 55-58. The lines are quoted from the 1696 edition of the *New Version;* in 1698 those quoted from Psalm 37 were rewritten, and "deserv'd" was altered to "dismal" in Psalm 91. But the references to "Tragedy" remained.

25. Quoted by E. K. Chambers, *The Mediaeval Stage* (Oxford, 1903), I, 11.

26. *A Defence of the Book of Psalms,* p. 64.

27. *An Essay for Promoting of Psalmody* (London, 1710), p. 17

28. *Ibid.*, p. 33.

29. *Ibid.*, pp. 4, 18, 24.

30. *Ibid.*, pp. 20-21.

31. The generalization of A. R. Humphreys, *The Augustan World*

(London, 1954), p. 138.

32. *An Essay for Promoting of Psalmody,* p. 28.

33. I. Watts, *The Psalms of David Imitated in the Language of the New Testament* (London, 1719), p. xvi.

34. (1915, reprinted Richmond, Va., 1962), pp. 46-63, esp. pp. 50-51.

Chapter Nine

1. Those who have preferred it to the rest of Tate's work include Broadus, *The Laureateship,* p. 101, and W. Forbes Gray, *The Poets Laureate of England* (New York, 1915), p. 108, who calls it his "masterpiece."

2. See Richmond P. Bond, *English Burlesque Poetry 1700-1750* (Cambridge, Mass., 1932), esp. pp. 108-9, 163-64, 238-39.

3. Motteux's poem was dedicated to the *Spectator,* and was acknowledged by Steele on December 3, 1712 (No. 552); it was reprinted in *The Bee,* Part III (London, 1715), pp. 38-46.

4. William H. Ukers, *All About Tea* (New York, 1935), I, 39-40.

5. *A Poem upon Tea,* 2nd ed. (London, 1702), p. 2.

6. *Ibid.,* p. 16.

7. *Ibid.,* pp. 21-22.

Selected Bibliography

PRIMARY SOURCES

1. Verse and Prose (separate publications)

Poems. London: B. Tooke, 1677.

A Poem on the Present Assembling of the Parliament March the 6th, 1678 [New Style, 1679]. London: n.p., 1679.

The Second Part of Absalom and Achitophel. London: J. Tonson, 1682.

Poems Written on several Occasions . . . The Second Edition enlarged. London: B. Tooke, 1684.

The Prologue [and Epilogue] To the last new Play A Duke and no Duke. London: G. Croom, 1684.

A Song for St. Cæcilia's Day 1685. London: n.p., [1685].

On the Sacred Memory of Our Late Sovereign: With a Congratulation to His Present Majesty. London: H. Playford (2 eds.), and Dublin, 1685.

A Pastoral Elegy On the Death of Mr. John Playford. London: H. Playford, 1687.

A Pastoral in Memory of his Grace The Illustrious Duke of Ormond. London: R. Taylor, 1688.

The Prolouge [sic] *to King William & Queen Mary*. London: R. Baldwin, 1689.

A Pastoral Dialogue. A Poem. London: R. Baldwin, 1690, 1691. Also published under the title *A Poem Occasioned by the Late Discontents & Disturbances in the State. With Reflections Upon the Rise and Progress of Priest-craft*. London, 1691.

A Poem, Occasioned by His Majesty's Voyage to Holland, The Congress at the Hague, and Present Siege of Mons. London: R. Baldwin, 1691.

Characters of Vertue and Vice . . . Attempted in Verse from a Treatise of the Reverend Joseph Hall. London: F. Saunders, 1691.

A Present for the Ladies: Being an Historical Vindication of the Female Sex. To which is added, The Character of an Accomplish'd Virgin, Wife, and Widow, in Verse. London: F. Saunders, 1692. 2nd ed., 1693.

An Ode upon the New-Year Performed Before their Majesties. London: R. Baldwin, 1693.

Ode upon Her Majesty's Birth-Day, April the Thirtieth. London: R. Baldwin, 1693.

An Ode upon the Ninth of January 1693/4. The First Secular Day Since the University of Dublin's Foundation by Queen Elizabeth. Dublin: J. Ray, 1694.

An Ode upon His Majesty's Birth-Day. London: R. Baldwin, 1694.

In Memory of Joseph Washington, Esq; Late of the Middle Temple, An Elegy. London: R. Baldwin, 1694.

A Poem on the Late Promotion of Several Eminent Persons in Church and State. London: R. Baldwin, 1694.

An Elegy on the Most Reverend Father in God, His Grace, John, Late Lord Archbishop of Canterbury. London: B. Aylmer and W. Rogers, 1695. Also published under the title *An Elegy on His Grace John, the Late Archbishop of Canterbury.* London: J. Whitlock, 1695.

Mausolæum: A Funeral Poem On Our Late Gracious Sovereign Queen Mary of Blessed Memory. London: B. Aylmer *et al.*, 1695.

The Anniversary Ode for the Fourth of December, 1697. His Mejesty's Birth-Day. Another for New-Year's-Day, 1697/8. Both Set to Musick, and Perform'd at Kensington. London: R. Baldwin, 1698.

A Consolatory Poem To the Right Honourable John Lord Cutts, Upon the Death of His Most Accomplish'd Lady. 2 eds., London: H. Playford, 1698.

A Proposall for Regulating of the Stage & Stage-Plays. Manuscript, Lambeth Palace, dated February 6, 1699. [Not seen.]

Elegies . . . Together with A Poem on the Promotion of Several Eminent Persons. London: J. Wild, 1699. The elegies are those for the Duke of Ormonde, the Countess of Dorset, Archbishop Tillotson, Queen Mary, and Lady Cutts.

An Essay of a Character Of the Right Honourable Sir George Treby Kt. London: R. Roberts for the Author, 1699.

Funeral Poems . . . Together with A Poem on the Promotion of Several Eminent Persons. London: J. Gardyner, 1700. The same contents as *Elegies.*

Panacea: A Poem upon Tea: In Two Canto's. London: J. Roberts, 1700. 2nd ed., *A Poem upon Tea.* London, 1702.

An Elegy in Memory of the Much Esteemed and truly Worthy Ralph Marshall, Esq; one of His Majesty's Justices of the Peace, &c. London: R. Roberts for the Author, 1700.

A Congratulatory Poem on the New Parliament Assembled on This Great Conjuncture of Affairs. London: W. Rogers, 1701. 2nd ed. advertised.

The Kentish Worthies. A Poem. London: A. Baldwin, 1701.

An Ode upon the Assembling of the New Parliament. Sung before His Majesty on New-Years-day, 1702. London: n.p., 1702.

A Letter to the Honoured Cavendish Weedon, Esq. London: H. Playford, 1702. [Not seen.]

A Monumental Poem in Memory of The Right Honourable Sir George Treby Kt. . . . Consisting of His Character and Elegy. London: J. Nutt, 1702.

The Song for New-Years-Day, 1703. Perform'd before Her Majesty. London: [J. Nutt], 1703.

Portrait-Royal. A Poem upon Her Majesty's Picture Set up in Guild-Hall. London: J. Nutt, 1703.

The Triumph, or Warriours Welcome: A Poem on the Glorious Successes Of the Last Year. With the Ode for New-Year's Day. 1705. London: J. Holland, 1705.

The Song for New-Year's-Day, 1706. [London, 1706].

Britannia's Prayer for the Queen. London: J. Chantry, 1706.

The Triumph of Union: With the Muse's Address For the Consummation of it in the Parliament of Great Britain. London: n.p., 1707.

The Song for the New-Year 1708. [London, 1708]. [Not seen.]

A Congratulatory Poem to His Royal Highness Prince George of Denmark . . . To which is added A Happy Memorable Song, on the Fight near Audenarde. London: H. Hills, 1708. Also published under the title *The Muse's Memorial of His Royal Highness, Prince George of Denmark.* London, 1708.

An Essay for Promoting of Psalmody. London: J. Holland, 1710.

The Song for Her Majesty's Birth-day, February the 6th 1710/11. London, 1711. [Not seen.]

The Muse's Memorial, Of the Right Honourable Earl of Oxford. London: J. Baker, 1712. 2nd ed. advertised at the end of *The Muse's Bower.*

The Muse's Bower, An Epithalamium on The Auspicious Nuptials of the . . . Marquis of Caermarthen, with the Lady Elizabeth

Harley. London: The Author, 1713.

The Triumph of Peace. A Poem. London: J. Holland, 1713.

A Congratulatory Poem on Her Majesties Happy Recovery, and Return to Meet Her Parliament. London: J. Holland, 1714.

A Poem Sacred to the Glorious Memory of Her Late Majesty Queen Anne. London: n.p., 1716.

2. Dramatic Works

Brutus of Alba: or, The Enchanted Lovers. London: J. Tonson, 1678.

The Loyal General, A Tragedy. London: H. Bonwicke, 1680.

The History of King Richard the Second Acted at the Theatre Royal, Under the Name of the Sicilian Usurper. With a Prefatory Epistle in Vindication of the Author. Occasion'd by the Prohibition of this Play on the Stage. London: R. and J. Tonson, 1681. Reissued under the title *The Sicilian Usurper.* London: S. Knapton, 1691.

The History of King Lear. London: E. Flesher, 1681. New eds. in 1689, 1699, [1702], and 1712.

The Ingratitude of a Common-Wealth: Or, The Fall of Caius Martius Coriolanus. London: J. Hindmarsh, 1682.

A Duke and no Duke. A Farce. London: H. Bonwicke, 1685. 2nd ed. with much enlarged Preface, 1693.

Cuckolds-Haven: or, An Alderman No Conjurer. A Farce. London: E. Poole, 1685.

The Island-Princess. London: W. Canning, 1687.

[Dido and Aeneas]. *An Opera Perform'd at Mr. Josias Priest's Boarding-School at Chelsey. By Young Gentlewomen. The Words Made by Mr. Nat. Tate. The Musick Composed by Mr. Henry Purcell.* London, [ca. 1690].

Injur'd Love: or, The Cruel Husband. London: R. Wellington, 1707.

The Constant Gallant or Truth found out at Last. A Comedy Being a Loose Translation of Terence's Andr[ia] Adapted to the humour of the English Stage a[s] farr as is Consistent with keeping the Origin[al] in View. Revised and Corrected by Nahum Tate Esq. late Poet Laureate to his Majesty. Manuscript, Folger Shakespeare Library, ca. 1765.

3. Translations

Ovid's Epistles, Translated by Several Hands. London: J. Tonson, 1680. Tate translated "Leander to Hero," "Hero's Reply to

Leander," and "Medea to Jason." Later editions in 1681, 1683, 1688, 1693, 1701, 1705, 1712.

Heliodorus of Emesa. *The Æthiopan History of Heliodorus. In Ten Books.* London: E. Poole, 1686. "A Person of Quality" translated the first five books, Tate the last five. 2nd ed. as *The Triumphs of Love and Constancy.* London, 1687.

Fracastoro, Girolamo. *Syphilis: or, A Poetical History of the French Disease.* London: J. Tonson, 1686. Also published in Part III of John Dryden, ed., *Miscellany Poems.* London, 1693.

Cowley, Abraham. *The Third Part of the Works of Mr Abraham Cowley, Being His Six Books of Plants . . . Now made English by several Hands.* London: C. Harper, 1689. Tate translated Books IV and V and wrote the dedication. Later editions in 1700, 1708, and 1711.

Coste, Pierre. *The Life of Lewis of Bourbon, Late Prince of Conde. Digested into Annals.* 2 vols. London: T. Goodwin, 1693.

The Satires of Decimus Junius Juvenalis. Translated into English Verse. By Mr. Dryden, and Other Eminent Hands. London: J. Tonson, 1693. Tate translated Satires II and XIV. Also published in 1697, 1702, 1711, 1713.

[Trial editions of five and eight Psalms. London? 1694?]

An Essay of a New Version of the Psalms of David: Consisting Of the first Twenty. Fitted to the Tunes used in Churches. London: Stationers Co., 1695. With Nicholas Brady.

An Essay of a New Version of the Psalms of David, Consisting of the first Seventy. London: Stationers Co., 1695. With Brady.

A New Version of the Psalms of David, Fitted to the Tunes Used in Churches. 2 eds., London: Stationers Co., 1696. With Brady. Two different revisions appeared in 1698; many later editions.

Ovid's Metamorphosis. Translated By Several Hands. Vol. I. London: W. Rogers *et al.*, 1697. Contains Books I-V, apparently all that were published. Tate signed the Epistle Dedicatory and translated two sections of Book IV.

A Supplement to the New Version of Psalms by N. Tate and N. Brady. London: J. Heptinstall, 1700. Many later editions.

Maidwell, Lewis. *Majestas Imperii Britannici. The Glories of Great Britain Celebrated in Latin Poems by Mr. Maidwell, Paraphras'd in English by Mr. Tate.* Part I. London: n.p., 1706.

The Celebrated Speeches of Ajax and Ulysses, for the Armour of Achilles. In the 13th Book of Ovid's Metamorph[oses]. Essay'd in English Verse by Mr. Tate, Poet Laureat; And Aaron Hill,

Gent. London, 1708. Tate translated Ajax's speech.

Ovid's Art of Love. In Three Books. Together with his Remedy of Love. London: J. Tonson, 1709. Dryden, Congreve, and another person translated the *Art*; Tate translated the *Remedy.* Also published in 1712.

The Works of Lucian, Translated from the Greek by Several Eminent Hands. 4 vols. London, 1710-11. Tate translated "Dialogues of the Gods: To Ridicule the Fables about Them," in IV, 233-83.

4. Editions

Poems by Several Hands, and on Several Occasions Collected by N. Tate. London: J. Hindmarsh, 1685. Includes translation of three "Piscatory Eclogues" of Sanazarius by Tate.

D., J., Gent. *A Memorial for the Learned; or, Miscellany of Choice Collections from [the] most Eminent Authors.* London: G. Powell and W. Powle, 1686.

Curtius Rufus, Quintus. *The Life of Alexander the Great. . . . Translated into English by several Gentlemen in the University of Cambridge.* London: F. Saunders, 1690.

Petty, Sir William. *The Political Anatomy of Ireland.* London: D. Brown and W. Rogers, 1691.

Boyle, Roger, Earl of Orrery. *Guzman.* London: F. Saunders, 1693.

Busbeq, Ogier G. de. *The Four Epistles of A. G. Busbequius, Concerning His Embassy into Turkey . . . To Which Is Now Added, His Advice How to Manage War against the Turks.* London: J. Taylor and J. Wyat, 1694.

Miscellanea Sacra; or, Poems on Divine and Moral Subjects. Vol. I. London: H. Playford, 1696. Republished in 1698 with additions and in 1705.

S., J. *The Innocent Epicure: or, The Art of Angling. A Poem.* London: S. Crouch *et al.*, 1697. 2nd ed., 1713.

Sheffield, John, Duke of Buckingham. *An Essay on Poetry.* 3rd ed. London: F. Saunders, 1697.

Davies, John. *The Original, Nature, and Immortality of the Soul. A Poem.* London: W. Rogers, 1697. Also published in 1699, 1714, 1715.

An Entire Set of the Monitors. . . . Containing Forty One Poems On Several Subjects. . . . Perform'd by Mr. Tate, Poet Laureat to Her Majesty, Mr. Smith, and Others. London, [1713]. This consists of the twenty-one numbers of the periodical bound together; Smith published a second edition in octavo, [1715?].

5. Complimentary Verses and Poems First Published in Collections or Periodicals.

Flatman, Thomas. *Poems and Songs.* 2nd ed. London: B. Took and B. Edwards, 1676. Complimentary verses by Tate.

[Dickinson, Henry], tr. *A Critical History of the Old Testament.* London: J. Tonson, 1682. Complimentary verses.

[Dryden, John]. *Absalom and Achitophel.* 3rd ed. London: J. T[onson], 1682. Complimentary verses.

[Dryden, John]. *The Medall.* London: J. Tonson, 1682. Complimentary verses.

[Creech, Thomas], tr. *T. Lucretius Carus. The Epicurean Philosopher, His Six Books De Natura Rerum Done into English Verse.* London, 1683. Complimentary verses.

Oldham, John. *Remains of Mr. John Oldham in Verse and Prose.* London: J. Hindmarsh, 1684. "In memory of the Author" by Tate.

Fane, Sir Francis. *The Sacrifice.* London: J. Weld, 1686. Complimentary verses.

Wright, John Michael. *An Account of His Excellence Roger, Earl of Castlemaine's Embassy.* London: T. Snowden, 1688. "Upon the foregoing Account of his Excellence the Earl of Castlemaine's Embassy Extraordinary to Rome, Anno 1687" and a brief translation of an Italian poem, both by Tate, pp. 113-16.

Harris, Joseph. *The Mistakes.* London: J. Hindmarsh, 1691. Epilogue by Tate.

Gildon, Charles. *The History of the Athenian Society.* London: J. Dowley, [1691]. "To the Athenian Society" by Tate.

The Gentleman's Journal; Or, The Monthly Miscellany:

"On Their Majesties Pictures drawn by the Life, by Mr. Kneller," January, 1692, pp. 2-4.

"Ænigma," April, 1692, p. 21.

"Verses to a Gentleman who was married very young," May, 1692, p. 11.

"The Anatomy," January, 1693, pp. 120-21.

"To the Publisher of the Translation of Rabelais," November, 1693, pp. 380-82.

Other poems by Tate that were also published separately appear in December, 1692, pp. 2-3 and 32-33; April, 1693, pp.

120-21 and 133-35; November, 1693, pp. 359-60; January-February, 1694, pp. 25-26; and October-November, 1694, pp. 269-70.

[Playford, Henry]. *Harmonia Sacra. . . . The Second Book.* London: H. Playford, 1693. "The Blessed Virgin's Expostulation" and "An Hymn upon the Last Day" by Tate.

The Temple of Death, A Poem. . . . Together with Several Other Excellent Poems. 2nd ed. London: F. Saunders, 1695. Includes an abbreviated version of Tate's elegy on the Countess of Dorset.

Orpheus Britannicus. London: H. Playford, 1698. Includes "A Lamentation for the Death of Mr. Henry Purcell" by Tate.

Ovington, J[ohn]. *A Voyage to Suratt, in the Year, 1689.* London: J. Tonson, 1696. Includes "To Mr. J. Ovington, on his Voyage to Suratt" by Tate.

Weedon, Cavendish. *The Oration, Anthems and Poems, Spoken and Sung at the Performance of Divine Musick. For the Entertainment of the Lords Spiritual & Temporal, And the Honourable House of Commons. At Stationers-Hall, January the 31st 1701.* London: H. Playford, 1602 [for 1702]. The two poems are by Tate.

Read, Thomas, ed. *The Penman's Magazine.* London: T. Read, 1705. "Upon this Performance of Penmanship" by Tate. Also published separately.

Maidwell, Lewis. *Nova Grammatices Experimeta: or, Some New Essays of a Natural and Artificial Grammar. . . with a Paraenetic Poem by Mr. Tate.* London: J. Burrough and J. Baker, 1707.

The Muses Mercury:

"Song. For the Performance of Musick at York buildings on the Thanksgiving-Day, December the 31st, 1706," January, 1707, pp. 7-8.

"Song for New-Year's Day, 1707," *ibid.*, pp. 8-9.

"Song for Her Majesty's Birth-Day, February the 6th, 1707," February, 1707, pp. [27]-28.

The Spectator, No. 488 (September 19, 1712). "On the Spectator" by Tate.

[Smith, M.] *Memoirs of the Mint and Queen's-Bench, . . . with . . . a Poem to the Marshall by Mr. Tate.* London, 1713.

Flying Post, June 9-11, 1715. "Song on His Majesty's Birth-Day, May 28, 1715" by Tate.

Two writings sometimes attributed to Tate are not his. *Macbeth: A Tragedy; As it is now Acted at the New Theatre in Edinburgh. Written by Mr. Shakespear, with Alterations by Mr. Tate* (Edinburgh, 1731) is Davenant's adaptation. It is incredible that *Apotheosis Basilike; or, A Pindarick Ode, Upon the Pious and Blessed Transit Of that most Excellent Prince James the II . . . Written at the Court of St. Germains in the . . . Year, 1701* (n.p., 1708) should have been written by King William's poet laureate, who would hardly have been welcome at Saint Germains in 1701, even if he had wished to go there.

SECONDARY SOURCES

1. Biographical and General

BENNETT, H. L. "Tate, Nahum," in *Dictionary of National Biography*. Vol. XIX. London: Oxford University Press, 1899, pp. 379-80. A brief account; Bennett mistakenly gives the date of Tate's death as August 12, 1715.

BROADUS, EDMUND K. *The Laureateship: A Study of the Office of Poet Laureate in England with Some Account of the Poets*. Oxford: Clarendon Press, 1921. Discusses Tate's tenure as Laureate and criticizes his official poems.

GOLDEN, SAMUEL A. "The Late Seventeenth Century Writer and the Laureateship: Nahum Tate's Tenure," *Hermathena*, LXXXIX (May, 1957), 30-38. Primarily concerned with Tate's financial difficulties.

———. "Nahum Tate." Doctoral thesis, Trinity College, Dublin, [1954]. A useful discussion of Tate's life and work, with a full bibliography; especially useful on Tate's father and grandfather, and on the poet's attendance at Trinity College.

———. The Three Faithful Teates," *Notes and Queries*, CC (1955), 374-80. Distinguishes among Tate's grandfather, father, and brother.

———. "Variations in the Name of Nahum Tate," *Notes and Queries*, CCI (1956), 72. On both first and last names.

GRAY, W. FORBES. *The Poets Laureate of England: Their History and Their Odes*. New York: Dutton, 1915. Biography with some critical comment; rather superficial.

HOPKINS, KENNETH. *The Poets Laureate.* New York: Library Publishers, 1955. A ten-page biography and six poems.

SCOTT-THOMAS, H. F. "The Date of Nahum Tate's Death," *Modern Language Notes,* XLIX (1934), 169-71. Corrects previous errors and confusions, and confirms July 30, 1715, as the date.

———. "The Life and Works of Nahum Tate." Doctoral dissertation, 2 vols., Johns Hopkins, 1932. Very detailed critical discussions, especially of the plays and non-Shakespearean adaptations; elaborate appendices comparing the adaptations with the originals.

———. "Nahum Tate and the Seventeenth Century," *A Journal of English Literary History,* I (1934), 250-75. Mostly the last chapter of his dissertation; the best discussion of Tate in relation to his age.

———. "Nahum Tate, Laureate: Two Biographical Notes," *Modern Language Notes,* LVI (1941), 611-12. Tate had a weak constitution; and in 1706 he tried to obtain the patronage of Charles Howard, Third Earl of Carlisle, whose father had supported him earlier.

SEYMOUR, ST. JOHN D. "Faithful Teate," *Journal of the Royal Society of Antiquaries of Ireland,* 6th Series, X (1920), 39-45. On the poet's grandfather and father, with some account of the father's writings.

2. Verse

FAIRCHILD, HOXIE N. *Religious Trends in English Poetry.* Vol. I: 1700-40. New York: Columbia University Press, 1939. Tate as religious poet, principally his contributions to *Miscellanea Sacra* and *The Monitor.*

JULIAN, JOHN, ed. *Dictionary of Hymnology.* Rev. ed. London: John Murray, 1907. Contains much information on the Psalters: see especially "Psalters, English," Section XIII; and "New Version."

"The Poems of Nahum Tate," *More Books: The Bulletin of the Boston Public Library,* 6th Series, XIII (1938), 152. Brief comment on *Poems* of 1677; the library's copy has Charles Cotton's autograph.

3. Drama

AYRES, JAMES B. "Shakespeare in the Restoration: Nahum Tate's *The History of King Richard the Second, The History of King Lear,* and *The Ingratitude of a Common-Wealth.*" Doctoral dissertation, Ohio State University, 1964. The principal topics discussed are the influence of politics, theory and practice in the application of Neoclassical "rules," the "language of statement," and alterations "for stage effectiveness."

GOLDEN, SAMUEL A. "An Early Defense of Farce." *Studies in Honor of John Wilcox.* Ed. A. D. Wallace and W. O. Ross. Detroit: Wayne State University Press, 1958, pp. 61-70. Sets Tate's 1693 Preface to *A Duke and No Duke* in its historical context and comments on it and, briefly, the play.

HODSON, GEOFFREY. "The Nahum Tate 'Lear' at Richmond," *Drama,* No. 81 (Summer, 1966), pp. 36-39. On the performance of Tate's adaptation at the Georgian Theatre, Richmond, in the spring of 1966.

HOLST, IMOGEN, ed. *Henry Purcell 1659-1695: Essays on His Music.* London: Oxford University Press, 1959. Contains "Purcell's Librettist, Nahum Tate" by the editor, pp. 35-41, and "New Light on Dido and Aeneas," with comment on Tate's libretto by E. W. White, pp. 14-34.

HUGHES, LEO, and A. H. SCOUTEN, eds. *Ten English Farces.* Austin: The University of Texas Press, 1948. Contains the text of *A Duke and No Duke* (without the 1693 Preface) and an introduction.

LEECH, CLIFFORD. *John Webster A Critical Study.* London: The Hogarth Press, 1951. Brief discussion of Tate's *Injur'd Love,* remarking especially on inconsistencies in the adaptation.

MCGUGAN, RUTH E. "Nahum Tate and the Coriolanus Tradition in English Drama with a Critical Edition of Tate's *The Ingratitude of a Common-Wealth.*" Doctoral dissertation, University of Illinois, 1965. In addition to the play, contains chapters on Tate, the adaptation of Shakespeare for the Restoration stage, and the "Coriolanus Tradition" before and after Tate, as well as a detailed discussion of Tate's adaptation.

MOORE, ROBERT E. *Henry Purcell & the Restoration Theatre.* Cambridge: Harvard University Press, 1961. Valuable for its discussion of the background of *Dido and Aeneas* and of Purcell's music for the opera.

SCOUTEN, ARTHUR H. "Aston Cokain and His Adapter Nahum Tate." Doctoral dissertation, Louisiana State University, 1942. Contains the texts of Cokain's *Trappolin* and Tate's *A Duke and No Duke* with historical, critical, and textual introductions for both, and explanatory notes.

———. "An Italian Source for Nahum Tate's Defence of Farce," *Italica,* XXVII (1950), 238-40. On Tate's use of Mariscotti in his Preface to *A Duke and No Duke.*

SHARKEY, PETER L. "Performing Nahum Tate's *King Lear:* Coming Hither by Going Hence," *Quarterly Journal of Speech,* LVI (1968), 398-403. On the performance of Tate's adaptation at Berkeley in 1967.

SPENCER, CHRISTOPHER, ed. *Five Restoration Adaptations of Shakespeare.* Urbana: University of Illinois Press, 1965. Includes a critical text of Tate's *King Lear,* with introduction, notes, and variants; also includes comments on Restoration adaptations in general.

———. "A Word for Tate's *King Lear,*" *Studies in English Literature 1500-1900,* III (1963), 241-51. Critical defense of the adaptation.

SPENCER, HAZELTON. *Shakespeare Improved.* Cambridge: Harvard University Press, 1927. Chapter VII contains a scene-by-scene analysis, critical comment, and discussion of the style of Tate's three Shakespeare adaptations.

———. "Tate and *The White Devil,*" *A Journal of English Literary History,* I (1934), 235-49. The same kind of discussion for Tate's adaptation of Webster's play.

SPRAGUE, ARTHUR COLBY. *Beaumont and Fletcher on the Restoration Stage.* Cambridge: Harvard University Press, 1926. Contains a discussion, like H. Spencer's, of the three Restoration adaptations of *The Island Princess.*

SUMMERS, MONTAGUE, ed. *Shakespeare Adaptations.* Boston: Small, Maynard and Company, 1922. Contains a rather inaccurate text of Tate's *King Lear,* with notes and an introduction on the adaptations.

Index